KEYS *TO AVOIDING*
DECEPTION
Keys For Living

God bless you
Huntley Brown

HUNTLEY BROWN

Keys To Avoiding Deception
Keys for Living
Huntley Brown

Huntley Brown Ministries
Website: http://huntleybrown.org
E-mail: huntley@huntleybrown.org

2112 West Galena Boulevard, Suite A285
Aurora, Illinois 60506
U.S.A.
630 907 0537

Copyright © 2017
ISBN 978-1-943342-56-3

PublishAffordably.com
www.PublishAffordably.com | 773-783-2981

DEDICATION

This book is dedicated to my parents Myrtle and Alpheus Brown. Thank you for teaching me the importance of knowing God for myself and not to be influenced by the culture but by the Word of God.

Thank you to:

My wife Annette and our four daughters Natalie, Natasha, Nicole, and Nadia. Thank you for your endless support and prayers.

My brothers Lenworth and Phillip, thank you for encouraging me in the pursuit of my dreams.

My Bible study group who has been a constant source of strength. Thank you for allowing me to be your teacher and also for being such an integral part of my pastoral journey: Dave and Priscilla Ferguson, Bob Springstroh, Russel and Judy Rhetter, Patti Austin, Bobette Keasler, Matthew, Jennie, Vinny, and Gabby Nardone, Timothy Tokars, Lucy Cerny, Bob and Holly Mack, Annette Brown, Esther Anderson, Phyllis Wells, Paul and Kathy Viney, Jim Hendricks, and Chuck Gillette.

Special thanks to Dr. Nina Bissett, Amy Roth, Randy York, Yvonne Coke, Roscoe and Revita Dechalus, Ye Kengale,

Agorom Dike, Lora Woodall and John Nieukerchen, for proof reading and all your editing help.

Special thanks to Marilyn Alexander, of PublishAffordably. com, who was very instrumental in the editing process. Thanks for your endless hours of hard work.

Additional thank you: Laruth Brown, Crystal Hamilton, Nevaeh Hamilton, Daphne Brown, Peter Knight, Tony and Martha Cimmarusti, Albina Paul, Greg Hare, Pat Hare, Matthew Hare, Ruth Graham, Jerry and Shirley Rose, Dr. Warren Anderson, Manny Mills, Dr. Eugene and Marie Frost, Joe and Sharon Ritchie, Joye Welsh, Barb Williams, Pastor Bill and Fran McMillan, Jim and Mary Whitmer, Larry and Connie Blaney, Dan and Gayle Haas, Carolyn Hanson, Dan and Sherri Gillette, Barb Williams, Susan Starratt, and Ralph and Joan Ferrante.

FOREWORD

Why write a book on deception—such a negative subject?

A few years ago I encountered a few verses in the Bible that shook me to the core. These verses should scare everyone and cause all of us to do some healthy introspection. They cover deception and are some of the most frightening verses in the Bible.

Once I uncovered those verses, I decided to take a serious look at myself and ask, "What do I need to do to guard against deception?"

The world has changed. We are now living in an upside down world—a world in which there are no clear lines of demarcation separating right from wrong. Right and wrong are no longer decided by God. It's now based on political correctness. This always leads to deception.

All great nations that fell were never conquered. They were destroyed from within; basically, an implosion took place. History proves that any society that operates without moral boundaries collapses sooner or later. Once there is a breakdown in moral clarity, deception happens, and society is destroyed.

God's rules are not meant to punish but to bless us and to establish order. A stoplight is a good thing because there are many people approaching the intersection from four angles with many different mindsets. Tragically many have been killed and many have killed others because they decided that the rules that govern the stop light were not applicable to them.

It's the same with the rules God has established. Without rules society will dissipate into the abyss of pandemonium leading to deception. Many call it the new normal. This new normal has been tried before, and it does not work.

With the new normal there are no moral absolutes. Moral boundaries have been thrown out and replaced with relativity. The basic premises are live and let live, whatever feels good do it, freedom of expression, freedom from God, and freedom to do whatever you like.

With this new normal, man tries to create God in his own image. As a result they have replaced God with a man-made version, which is no God at all.

God in His wisdom allows people who subscribe to this thinking to take their own journey. He knows that sooner or later they will wake up to the reality that He knew what He was doing.

This book purposely has two titles because I believe if I am going to outline a problem, I should at least be able to make some suggestions or recommend a solution.

This book is an attempt to alert people to the danger of deception. As a result, I try to address it from many angles. My prayer is that each person who reads this book will be challenged, inspired, and blessed at the same time. May God bless you as you read.

Huntley Brown

TABLE OF CONTENTS

PART TWO

PART THREE

INTRODUCTION

How can this be?

I watched him preach, and he was anointed.

He was one incredible preacher, singer, and musician. When he preached, sang, or played, everyone got goose bumps and said they felt the presence of the Lord.

I saw him cast out demons and heal the sick. The power of the Lord was very evident in his life.

He took care of the poor and was greatly involved in the church. Whenever problems surfaced, he was there leading the charge with solutions. He gave generously to the poor and took care of widows and orphans. He visited those in prison and conducted major evangelistic campaigns to spread the gospel.

Am I hearing right?

Did Jesus just say to him, "Depart from Me, I never knew you."?

Wow!

What happened?

What you have just read is not a fictional account. It is a prophetic declaration by Jesus warning us of the most dreadful day in the life of many people.

The Bible contains amazing verses. Verses of encouragement, rules for living, health, investing, behavior—you name it, it's all there. At the same time, there are many frightening verses. Here are a few:

> Matthew 7:21–23
> *Not everyone who says to me, 'Lord, Lord,' will enter the kingdom of heaven, but only the one who does the will of my Father who is in heaven. Many will say to me on that day, 'Lord, Lord, did we not prophesy in your name and in your name drive out demons and in your name perform many miracles?' Then I will tell them plainly, 'I never knew you. Away from me, you evildoers!*

After reading and rereading those verses, it is evident that these verses are not to be taken lightly. Out of great concern they led me to ask a few questions.

Who are these people?

What causes this level of deception?

How did these people get here?

These verses forced me to take an introspective look at myself and ask another question, "What do I need to do to guard against deception and make sure I never hear the words of Matthew 7:23, *'Depart from Me, I never knew you'*"?

Let's take a closer look and unpack these verses.

Jesus is saying there are many (that's scary because He used the word *many*) people who say they are Christians, believe they are, and convince themselves and others that they are, but they are not. They are living in full-blown deception and don't know it. That's why it's called deception.

They possess supernatural gifts and are spreading the gospel. They are prophesying, casting out demons, and performing miracles in the name of Jesus. They may be pastors, musicians, worship leaders, evangelists, or regular church members.

Jesus is telling us that many of these people are deceived, and their deception won't be exposed until He returns. That's a warning everyone should take very seriously.

Paul puts it this way:

> 1 Corinthians 9:27
> *"No, I strike a blow to my body and make it my
> slave so that after I have preached to others, I
> myself will not be disqualified for the prize."*

Paul is saying to himself, "I don't want to be deceived, so I have to be very careful. I don't want to spend my entire life preaching to others and then at the end hear that I have been disqualified."

We have all seen races at the Olympic Games when one runner seems to have won the race, but very shortly discovers he or she has been disqualified. Imagine spending years training for the Olympics and at the end of the race hearing the word "Disqualified."

No one wants to hear that word for a race that has no eternal significance. Just imagine hearing, "Depart from Me, I never knew you," after completing the race of life.

Many have correctly said that none of us know who is going to heaven. We can't see people's hearts. We cannot speak for anyone but ourselves.

It's also important to note that none of us can get to heaven on a family plan. With God there is no family plan.

On judgment day, God won't call the Brown family to stand together before Him. It's going to be each of us individually standing before a holy God, being judged by His rules, not our sincerity, emotions, tears, or good works. Good works are important, but God is looking for much more than good works to determine our eternal destiny.

I shudder to think that there are people who live their entire lives in deception and won't find out until the final day.

In Acts 20:28–31, the Apostle Paul gives us a warning:

> *Keep watch over yourselves and all the flock of which the Holy Spirit has made you overseers. Be shepherds of the church of God, which he bought with his own blood. I know that after I leave, savage wolves will come in among you and will not spare the flock. Even from your own number men will arise and distort the truth in order to draw away disciples after them. So be on your guard! Remember that for three years I never stopped warning each of you night and day with tears.*

There are warnings, and then there are *dire warnings.*

What could be so serious that it would cause Paul to warn people consistently for three years? What could be so serious that it would cause him to issue this warning night and day *with tears?*

A dire warning of this magnitude signifies that the person issuing the warning understands the monumental consequences of not heeding such a warning. This subject of deception is so serious that we can't approach it lightly.

So how do you guard against deception?

First, start with the premise that anyone can be deceived. We are all humans, and that means our ability to process information can be skewed by our own life experiences. **If we say we can't be deceived, that in itself is deception.** Start by accepting the fact that all of us can be deceived.

Second, by applying the 45 keys outlined in this book.

Keys For Living
PART ONE

KEYS TO AVOIDING DECEPTION

DISCERNMENT

It looks good, sounds good, feels good but something is telling me it is not good. What is that? That's the spirit of discernment, and we all need to pray for that gift in order to guard against deception.

The word *discern* comes from the Greek word *anakrino,* which basically means to examine, judge, sift, and distinguish. A spirit of discernment is an internal witness that allows us to bypass our physical senses. Having this ability enables one to say, "It looks good, sounds good, and feels good, but my discerning spirit says it's not good." It might pass the eye test, but with a spirit of discernment it won't pass the deception test.

Many people make decisions solely based on the eye test, which is dangerous because your eyes can deceive you. With a spirit of discernment, you will be able to get past the eye test and critically sift through the maze of information. This then allows the person to come to the right conclusion, which in turn affects their decision making.

With so many voices speaking and many claiming to be speaking for God, how do we know through whom God is really speaking? How do we guard against certain belief systems and teachings that can lead us to a place of deception? How do we know to whom we should listen?

Deceived, deluded, led astray, hoodwinked, tricked—these are words that cause fear in the hearts of people. They are all part of the deception family. These words are frightening because many times they are only discovered in retrospect, after the damage has been done.

"I was deceived. He led me astray. I believed a lie. I was tricked."

Have you ever been there? But what exactly does deception truly mean?

The dictionary describes it this way: *To cause to believe what is not true. To give a false impression. A ruse; a trick.*

To be deceived by others is terrible, but being deceived by one's own self is worse.

My definition of deception is **believing you are right when you are wrong, and you do not know it**.

It's such a serious word that the Bible warns us over and over again to guard against it.

> Matthew 24:4
> *"And Jesus answered and said unto them, Take heed that no man deceive you."*

> 1 John 1:8
> *"If we claim to be without sin, we deceive ourselves and the truth is not in us."*

> 1 Timothy 4:1
> *"The Spirit clearly says that in later times some will abandon the faith and follow deceiving spirits and things taught by demons."*

1 Corinthians 15:33 (ESV)
"Do not be deceived. Bad company ruins good morals."

Galatians 6:7
"Do not be deceived. God cannot be mocked. A man reaps what he sows."

James 1:22
"Do not merely listen to the word, and so deceive yourselves. Do what it says."

Matthew 24:24
"For there shall arise false Christs, and false prophets, and shall shew great signs and wonders; insomuch that, if it were possible, they shall deceive the very elect."

What a warning. Jesus is saying that if it were possible, the very elect could be deceived.

Throughout history, we have seen many examples of people who have been deceived. The deception highway is littered with the bodies of the deceived.

One pastor went on television and radio claiming he knew the exact date Jesus would return. His deception went so far that when his predictions did not come to pass, he revised the date and made a new prediction. As a result, he led thousands astray.

Many lost homes, money, friendships, and credibility, and are now disillusioned wondering what happened. Why were they not able to discern that this pastor was not telling the truth? How could they have been deceived? The simple answer is that they put their trust in the wrong person.

The Bible says in *Psalm 146:3, "Do not put your trust in princes, in human beings, who cannot save."*

We are also warned about trusting ourselves in *Proverbs 28:26*, "He who trusts in himself is a fool, but he who walks in wisdom is kept safe."

If we can't trust others or ourselves, who should we trust? In numerous places, the Bible tells us.

> Proverbs 3:5–6
> *Trust in the Lord with all your heart and lean not on your own understanding. In all thy ways acknowledge him, and he shall direct thy paths.*
>
> Psalm 40:4
> *Blessed is the one who trusts in the Lord, who does not look to the proud, to those who turn aside to false gods.*
>
> Psalm 118:8
> *It is better to take refuge in the Lord than to trust in humans.*

What caused this pastor to be so deceived? What caused so many people to fall for his deception?

The simple answer is this pastor did not believe the Scripture he read, and the people trusted the pastor more than they trusted the Word of God.

The pastor did the opposite of what we find in Scripture, and this led to his deception. The people were deceived because they failed to study the Word of God and believe it for themselves. The Scripture says, *"Study to shew thyself approved unto God, a workman that needeth not to be ashamed, rightly dividing the word of truth"* (2 Timothy 2:15).

If the people had studied Gods work they would have known this verse:

Mark 13:32
But about that day or hour no one knows, not even the angels in heaven, nor the Son, but only the Father.

If the Bible says no one knows, what part of *no one knows the day or hour* don't we understand? One has to wonder why the pastor and his followers would dismiss that verse. This explains the importance of owning your faith. This means working it out for yourself.

Know why you believe what you believe.

Don't say, "I believe this because my pastor believes it." Work it out for yourself. We are encouraged to do this in *Philippians 2:12, "Wherefore, my beloved, as ye have always obeyed, not as in my presence only, but now much more in my absence, work out your own salvation with fear and trembling."*

This pastor led the people into deception, and the people were deceived because they could not discern that this pastor was wrong. They needed to take the journey for truth that I took a few years ago.

While in graduate school, I interacted with many friends from other religions, a few agnostics, and some atheists. They thought I was deceived for being a Christian and were asking questions I could not answer. Praise God, I can answer their questions now, but at that time I had difficulty giving a clear answer.

The questions they asked included:

• How do you know there is a God?

5

- How do you know the Bible is true?

- How do you know the Bible has not been tampered with?

- Do all religions lead to God?

- Is Jesus the only way?

- Is there life after death?

- Is there really a hell?

Those questions were pivotal in my life because they forced me to go on a journey for truth.

To start the journey, I had a meeting with myself and asked a few honest questions.

- Why do I believe what I believe?

- How do I know if what I believe is true?

During this meeting, I discovered that my belief system was not based on my own critical thinking but on what I learned from my parents, pastors, brothers, teachers, and friends.

What if our beliefs were not true? How would I know for sure?

Simply accepting someone's belief system and claiming it as our own without really examining it can lead to deception.

The consequences of bad judgment—even though sincere—can be catastrophic.

I had to keep the following saying in mind, **"Always believing something does not make it right."** As a result, I decided to go on a journey to discover and solidify my own personal belief system.

Whatever belief system one subscribes to should be time-tested, verifiable, backed up by solid evidence, and able to sustain when difficult times arise. Answering life's most important questions using a flawed belief system inevitably leads to deception.

The journey was incredible, and as a result I know clearly why I believe what I believe. I also have enough evidence to support my own personal beliefs. Part of my own belief system is based on faith for sure, but on a foundational level, I discovered there is enough tangible evidence to support and help me solidify my own personal belief system.

This is supported in *Romans 1:18–20:*

> *The wrath of God is being revealed from heaven against all the godlessness and wickedness of people, who suppress the truth by their wickedness, since what may be known about God is plain to them, because God has made it plain to them. For since the creation of the world God's invisible qualities—his eternal power and divine nature—have been clearly seen, being understood from what has been made, so that people are without excuse.*

God is saying, "The proof of My existence is there for everyone to see. Just open your eyes and look around you."

At home, my wife and I tell our kids, "Don't simply take our word about God. Go on your own journey. Discover God for yourself." As a result, our children are free to challenge anything we tell them and praise God they do.

We have also given them a rule: If at any time we say anything that seems to contradict the Word of God, they have our permission to dismiss our opinion and go with the Word. We tell them no matter what they hear, no matter what laws are passed, no matter what their friends say, always go with the Word. The Word never changes. It's a solid rock on which you can build your lives that will help you to guard against deception.

When your pastor preaches, it's very important not to simply accept what he is teaching, but to examine it for yourself. This is what the Bereans were commended for. *"Now the Berean Jews were of more noble character than those in Thessalonica, for they received the message with great eagerness and examined the Scriptures every day to see if what Paul said was true" (Acts 17:11).*

There are many false teachers and if there ever was a time to guard against deception, it is now. We cannot say we have not been warned.

> 2 Peter 2:1–3
> *But there were also false prophets among the people, just as there will be false teachers among you. They will secretly introduce destructive heresies, even denying the sovereign Lord who bought them—bringing swift destruction on themselves. Many will follow their depraved conduct and will bring the way of truth into disrepute. In their greed these teachers will exploit you with fabricated stories. Their condemnation has long been hanging over them, and their destruction has not been sleeping.*

> 1 John 4:1
> *Dear friends, do not believe every spirit, but test the spirits to see whether they are from God,*

because many false prophets have gone out into the world.

Matthew 7:15
Watch out for false prophets. They come to you in sheep's clothing, but inwardly they are ferocious wolves.

I struggle to find words adequate enough to express how frightening those verses are.

It is also important to know that our friends, even though sincere, can mistake God's leading and lead us astray by their counsel. Peter was one of the closest friends of Jesus, and they had many conversations. Once Jesus asked him a question in *Matthew 16:15, "But what about you?" he asked. "Who do you say I am?"*

Peter responded:

Matthew 16:16
You are the Messiah, the Son of the living God.

In Matthew 16:17, Jesus replied,

Blessed are you, Simon son of Jonah, for this was not revealed to you by flesh and blood, but by my Father in heaven.

Peter was able to discern correctly by the Holy Spirit who Jesus is.

Do you discern things by the Holy Spirit?

If you do, what's the proof?

Jesus and Peter had another conversation, but this time Jesus rebuked Satan for trying to influence Peter.

> Matthew 16:22–23
> *Peter took him aside and began to rebuke him.*
> *Never, Lord! he said. This shall never happen to*
> *you! Jesus turned and said to Peter, Get behind*
> *me, Satan! You are a stumbling block to me;*
> *you do not have in mind the concerns of God,*
> *but merely human concerns.*

First, Peter was able to accurately discern through the power of the Holy Spirit that Jesus is the Messiah. The second time he was wrong because what he was hearing was from the devil.

Have you ever thought the Lord told you something only to discover later that you were wrong and God had not spoken? What do you do when that happens?

I believe you should go into a serious time of prayer and have an honest conversation with God. Ask Him to reveal to you exactly what happened. Ask Him to help you to learn from your mistakes and show you how to clearly hear His voice.

In closing this first key, I would like to pray a prayer for each person reading this book.

> Philippians 1:9–11
> *And this is my prayer: that your love may*
> *abound more and more in knowledge and depth*
> *of insight, so that you may be able to discern*
> *what is best and may be pure and blameless for*
> *the day of Christ, filled with the fruit of*
> *righteousness that comes through Jesus Christ—*
> *to the glory and praise of God.*

Key #1 Discernment

THE GOD FACTOR

Of all the questions that deserve careful study, this one should be at the top of the list.

Is there a God?

My atheist friends tell me, there is no God—that's deception.

To me, the question is not *if* there is a God. The question is, *who* is the true God because the evidence for God's existence is overwhelming. We cannot in good conscience look at the universe and say there is no God.

Someone created the heavens and the earth. It is impossible that the universe evolved by itself. I have told my atheist friends that they are being intellectually dishonest. Even though they disagree, the evidence is overwhelming.

Let's examine some facts about the universe. Scientists have discovered that the sun's core is about 13,000 degrees Fahrenheit. At the same time, we are 92 million miles away from it. Why *13,000 degree heat* with a *92 million mile human separation?* If the earth were any closer to the sun, we would all burn up, and if it was any further apart, we would all freeze to death. What are the chances of this happening by accident? A gazillion to one—meaning impossible.

Even when you are standing still, you are still moving because the earth is rotating on its axis.

Oxygen makes up about 21 percent of the atmosphere. Why 21 percent? If it were more, the first time someone started a fire, we would be no more.

The cycle of life in the wild could not happen by accident.

We can't even talk about the human body, because there is no way we could evolve. Just studying the eye, we will see there is a God.

The brain is far too complex to evolve. The creation narrative is one worth exploring by all humanity.

> Psalm 8:3
> *"When I consider thy heavens, the work of thy fingers, the moon and the stars, which thou hast ordained . . ."*

The universe is screaming, "Just look at me; this is all the evidence you need to verify the existence of God!"

The example I have used with my atheist friends is the airplane. Is it possible to throw a bunch of garbage outside and out comes an airplane? A 747 jet with two wings, luggage compartment, seats that recline, two trained pilots, a navigational system, entertainment system, coffee, your regular plus your decaf, fuel compartment, oxygen masks, lights, windows, and so on.

Is that possible?

We all know the answer is no.

The mathematical impossibility of the airplane coming into

existence by accident defies human logic. It's the same with the earth and the human body. We cannot in good conscience look at this amazing planet and the human body and say there is no God. If we do, we are deceiving ourselves.

The truth is, there is a God, and He does not need us to validate His existence.

What God has done is provide enough evidence for us to know that He exists. In my opinion, my atheist friends have chosen not to see the evidence for God. I believe it takes more faith to be an atheist than a Christian because the evidence for God is overwhelming.

That is why Scripture says man is without excuse. Romans 1:18–20 addresses this:

> *The wrath of God is being revealed from heaven against all the godlessness and wickedness of people, who suppress the truth by their wickedness, since what may be known about God is plain to them, because God has made it plain to them. For since the creation of the world God's invisible qualities—his eternal power and divine nature—have been clearly seen, being understood from what has been made, so that people are without excuse.*

The truth is, I cannot explain God. No one can.

How do you explain a God who has no beginning and no end? A God who created the universe and all humanity?

What we need to do is accept and believe what God has said and revealed about Himself. God has given us enough evidence for His existence. All we have to do is examine and believe the evidence. The truth is, the evidence is overwhelming. There is a God, and He is a rewarder of those who diligently seek Him.

> Hebrews 11:6
> *And without faith it is impossible to please God,*
> *because anyone who comes to Him must believe*
> *that He exist and that He rewards those who*
> *earnestly seek him.*

Are you genuinely seeking God?

If you are genuinely seeking God, you will find Him. Don't deceive yourself by being intellectually dishonest. Look at the evidence and call it what it is.

The truth is, God exists. He will reveal Himself to you if you are genuinely seeking Him with a pure heart.

> Jeremiah 29:13 NIV
> *You will seek me and find me when you seek me*
> *with all your heart.*

Key #2 The God Factor

LEARN TO HEAR THE VOICE OF GOD FOR YOURSELF

At home we teach our children that the most important thing they can do is learn to hear the voice of God for themselves.

I never want my family or anyone to believe something just because I said it. I want people to use their own critical thinking and analytical skills to sift the information and then draw their own conclusions. This allows a person to be an independent thinker. Independent thinkers with a solid godly foundation are not easily deceived. This is developed by learning to hear the voice of God for yourself.

How do you know for sure what God's will is?

Say you have a major decision to make and you want to know God's will. What do you do? Do you listen for an audible voice? Moses did. *Exodus 3.* Do you put out a fleece? Gideon did. *Judges 6:36–40.* Do you listen for a still, small voice? Elijah did. *1 Kings 19:11–13.* Do you look for signs and wonders?

> Mark 16:17–18
> *And these signs will accompany those who believe: In my name they will drive out demons; they will speak in new tongues; they will pick up snakes with their hands; and when they drink deadly poison, it will not hurt them at all; they*

will place their hands on sick people, and they will get well."

Signs and wonders are not bad, but we have to be really careful because there are many fake signs and wonders being displayed.

> 2 Thessalonians 2:9
> *The coming of the lawless one will be in accordance with the work of Satan displayed in all kinds of counterfeit miracles, signs and wonders.*

> Matthew 24:24
> *For false messiahs and false prophets will appear and perform great signs and wonders to deceive, if possible, even the elect.*

Do you listen to your mind, your spirit, or your emotions?

Do you just read the Word and then do whatever the Word says?

There are no verses that say become a pastor, a doctor, a nurse, a farmer, or a musician. So what do you do to hear God's voice? Implement this verse:

> Proverbs 3:6
> *In all thy ways acknowledge Him and He shall direct thy path."*

What does *all* mean?

It means *everything*. Since we know that God wants to be involved in every area of our lives, how do we know what is His will regarding the different situations we face?

What is the compass you use to determine God's will for your life?

God speaks in different ways. It is important to note that we cannot put God in a box and say this is the way He has to speak. Our responsibility is to train ourselves to recognize His voice.

How do you do this?

Here are seven steps to help us to recognize God's voice:

1. Training starts with having a personal relationship with Jesus Christ.

2. It is maintained by a daily study of the Bible. Read the Word! God speaks to us through His Word.

3. It is maintained by not only talking to God, but by listening to His voice. We need to make sure we are not the only one doing the talking. Prayer is a conversation. It is us communicating with God, and God communicating with us. Make sure it is not a one-sided conversation. Remember, hearing the voice of God for yourself won't happen overnight.

4. Make sure you are walking in full obedience to God.

5. Meditate: In silence, we get rid of distractions and can see and hear things we never knew or heard before.

6. Find a few people you trust spiritually and ask them to pray with you.

Many times, God will use others to confirm what He is telling you. After that, the evidence will be there for everyone to see.

A few years ago, I was ministering at a concert. A pastor and his wife attended and cried throughout the concert. A year later, I heard what really happened.

The pastor and his wife could not have children. With the recommendation from a friend and a Bible verse to stand on, they decided to step out in faith and trust God for a baby. They put out a fleece to God, which was this: If they heard the Bible verse their friend mentioned two more times that day, they would take that as a sign from God confirming they would have children. They wanted to hear the same verse three times.

They went to church in the morning and, without knowing about their fleece, their pastor mentioned the verse their friend mentioned. Finally, they came to my concert, and I also mentioned the verse. They cried through the rest of the concert. A year later, they had their baby.

7. Be patient. This won't happen overnight. But you have to start somewhere.

So how do you know for sure that you are hearing God's voice clearly?

Let's do an experiment.

You hear a thought inside your mind. You wonder, *Is this God or is this just me talking to myself, or is this from the devil?* Keep in mind the devil can also talk to you and deceive you into believing it was your idea.

Ideas can come from four places: God, the devil, yourself or others.

So you hear a thought. What do you do?

You test it by filtering it through the Word and in prayer.

Always remember that God will never contradict His Word.

Start with the Word. The Scripture says to walk by the Spirit, not by emotions. Never allow your emotions to guide you. Jesus said that He is going to lead us by our spirit.

> John 16:13
> *But when he, the Spirit of truth, comes, he will guide you into all the truth. He will not speak on his own; he will speak only what he hears, and he will tell you what is yet to come.*

Are you led by the Spirit? If you are, how do you know? Are there things in your life that you can look at and say, "This was not me; I was being led by the Spirit?"

In the beginning, many times you won't know until after the fact, and you look back in retrospect. In hindsight you will be able to know if God was leading or not. As time goes on, you will know for sure whether you were led by God.

Many years ago I got up and felt the need to fast and pray. I tried everything to talk myself out of the fast. My final excuse was my cereal was already soaked with milk, so I should not waste it. Just before taking my first bite, our daughter Natalie showed up and said, "Dad, can I have your cereal?" I took that as a final sign from God, so I obeyed and fasted.

At about 3 p.m., I got a call from my wife saying she had been in a major car accident and the air bags had deployed. The vehicle was totaled, but Annette and our kids were safe. Internally I heard the words, *now you understand why I wanted you to fast.*

A few years later I was on a cruise. One morning I got up and felt the need to fast. I talked myself out of this fast by saying, "No one fasts on a cruise." Those who have been on a cruise have seen the incredible spread of food on the ship. The temptation was great, and I succumbed to it. I then went and had a hearty breakfast.

Shortly after breakfast, I got sick. I mean *really* sick. I spent the next few days in bed wishing I had listened to my spirit.

Of all the times I have heard the Lord speak to me, one that really stands out is the journey the Lord allowed us to take with Covenant Christian School in Aurora, Illinois.

The school was going through a very difficult time and was in the process of closing. My friend, who was the pastor of the church and chairman of the school board, shared the bad news with me. The news was not a total surprise to me because earlier the Lord had spoken to my spirit about the possibility of this happening. I had put that conversation in the back of my mind, but with the new information, the Lord spoke again.

(I know a few people might be concerned with me saying the Lord spoke to me. They believe God does not speak like this anymore. I totally disagree. What I would recommend to my friends in this camp is to just keep reading and then draw your own conclusion if God truly spoke.)

This time the Lord spoke clearly and asked me about taking over the school. I asked my friend about turning the school over to me. He said, "Let me consult the board and get back to you."

I then went home and told my wife what I felt the Lord was asking me to do.

She took a serious look at me and asked a few poignant questions.

"Have you lost your mind?"

"Have you ever run a school?"

"Do you know what it really means to run a school?"

"Where are we going to get the money to pay the teachers?"

She knew I had no answers to all her questions, but she had to verbally communicate her words to make sure I understood the magnitude of the situation. My answer to all of the above was "No."

The truth was, I had no clue what I was doing. The only difference was, I knew the voice of God, and I knew He told me to offer to take over the school.

When the Lord spoke, He did not ask if I was qualified. He just wanted my availability.

As the saying goes, **"God never calls the qualified, he qualifies the called."**

Annette then outlined the reality of the situation. The school was closing because the recession had affected everyone, and the school could not pay the teachers.

The debt was thousands upon thousands of dollars and growing rapidly. We did not have the money to pay the teachers, so this would have to be an act of God.

More bad news was to come. My friend called and asked for a second meeting. Just before I went, the Lord spoke to me again.

Many times people ask, "When God speaks to you, what do you hear?" In my case, I do not hear an audible voice. What I hear is a thought in my spirit that's so strong I know it's the voice of God.

How do I know this? By years of testing the voice. In the early years I did not recognize this to be God's voice, but as the years went on, I tested the voice many times and very soon discovered it was indeed the Lord speaking.

Over the years I have told my family members and friends, "Don't take my word; examine the fruit. If the Lord truly spoke, the evidence will be there to back it up." As a result, I make sure I don't run around saying all the time, "The Lord told me this or that."

The name of the Lord has been discredited by people claiming "God said" when God never said. That's why it's important for all of us to walk with a spirit of humility and discernment.

This time I felt the Lord say, "You are going to a meeting, and you are going to get bad news, but don't worry. I have it covered." That's all I heard in my spirit.

I went to the meeting having no idea what I was going to hear, but I knew it was going to be bad. I got to the meeting and what I heard from the Lord was right—it was bad news compounded.

My friend told me the owner of the building housing the school decided to double the rent. Adding to the bad news, the electric bill had not been paid in quite some time, and so the company planned to turn off the lights the next week. With all the students with delinquent accounts, he thought the best option was to close the school.

I listened to all the bad but accurate news and told him not to worry. God had it covered.

Very soon the equation changed in our home with one conversation.

Annette said, "I disagree with you on this journey, but if you really feel God spoke to you, I will support you."

I can't stress the importance of husbands and wives walking in unity when dealing with various challenges. It is important to note here that **unity does not mean agreement**. Annette and I were not in agreement, but we united. This was pivotal in this journey. I told her, "Yes, God had indeed spoken," and to watch for the evidence.

Annette got sick right away and had to go to bed. She is an accountant and looking at the numbers, she understood the magnitude of the task at hand. With prayer, Annette recovered and was very instrumental in charting a course of action.

We agreed there was only one way this was going to work: we had to hear the voice of God clearly for ourselves and then walk in full obedience to His Word.

Accepting the dire consequences, the school board agreed and turned over the school to me. I remember signing all the legal papers realizing this was for real, but I was not scared because I knew God had spoken.

I called the principal and the staff, and we had a meeting. I told them I had no idea what I was doing but if they would stick with me, everyone would be paid.

They were all amazing and everyone stayed. The staff also agreed to go on a 21-day period of fasting and praying. God heard our prayers and honored the fast.

With God's help, we put a new board in place. I cannot express how amazing this board was. We did not always agree, which I believe was healthy, but we all kept our eyes on the goal. There was one board member with whom I clashed regularly. At the same time, I knew this member was sent by

God. Even though we did not see eye to eye, I recognized this member's strength and came to the conclusion that we could not have made it without that member's valuable contribution.

For all those putting boards together, don't get "yes" people around you. That's a recipe for deception and disaster. Get people around you that you trust even though you sometimes disagree. You should have the wisdom to know if what they are saying is sensible and useful.

At supernatural speed, the Lord found the school a new home and in a few days we had the entire school relocated.

I was happy and concerned at the same time. Happy because we were making progress, but concerned because the money needed to stabilize our financial condition was not forthcoming. To add to the confusion, most of our wealthy friends had turned us down.

Everything changed in December. I went to Michigan to meet with a wealthy friend and his wife. I explained to them the situation, and they wrote a check for $10,000. I was so excited! I felt we were now on the path to financial wholeness.

When I returned home, I discovered my joy was short lived. The principal told me this was a miracle because if that check had not come in, we would not have made payroll in December.

This frightened and woke me up at the same time. I then asked God to clearly show me what the problem was. Where was the blockage? I knew He had called me to lead the school, but where was the money? I know God spoke clearly, but why was I getting gray hairs and getting stressed out?

The Lord then gave me a vision of a bucket with holes in it.

The Lord made it clear that no matter how much water you

put in a bucket with holes, it's going to leak. Meaning, no matter how much money the Lord sends, because of the leak, we were going to be in the same financial position again. I shared that with the board, and we decided to take a microscopic look at the budget to identify the holes and plug them.

Once the holes were identified, we plugged them, and then the financial gates were opened. Friends in Taiwan, Atlanta, Michigan, California, Illinois, Georgia, Texas, plus many others sent money.

The Lord also gave me a revelation that one day we would have a *Berakah* celebration. I had never heard of a Berakah celebration before. I found the idea in 2 Chronicles 20 where a powerful story is told.

King Jehoshaphat was facing an army so large he knew they could not defeat them. I loved what Jehoshaphat did, so we decided to apply that to the school.

> 2 Chronicles 20 3–4, 12, NIV
> *Alarmed Jehoshaphat resolved to inquire of the Lord, and he proclaimed a fast for all Judah. The people of Judah came together to seek help from the Lord; Indeed they came from every town in Judah to seek Him. . . . O our God will you not judge them? For we have no power to face this vast army that is attacking us. We do not know what to do, but our eyes are upon you.*

The line that caught my attention was, "*We do not know what to do, but our eyes are upon you.*"

I plan to write a book one day called: *What to Do When You Don't Know What to Do.*

Jehoshaphat showed us what to do in 2 Chronicles 20:

1. First, he inquired of the Lord. We will cover this in depth in Key #19.

2. He issued a call for everyone to show up. The people came from every town, united in purpose.

3. Jehoshaphat prayed a powerful prayer reminding God who He is and of His promises.

4. He not only prayed, he had everyone fast. Some things can only be accomplished through prayer *and* fasting (*Mark 9:29*).

5. He ends by saying, *"We do not know what to do, but our eyes are on you."* In other words he was saying to God, "We are looking to You for the answer."

6. Everyone then listened for God to give instructions.

7. Once they heard from God, they gave thanks and then walked in full obedience to the instructions they got from the Lord.

We can learn a lot from the actions of Jehoshaphat and the people.

They were united while waiting with anticipation and expectancy.

The power of unity in a crisis cannot be overemphasized.

The people did not tell God what to do or through whom to speak. When you do not know what to do, you must trust God for His answer. Our responsibility is to ask God in faith and then wait for the avenue God chooses to answer our request.

God answered the people through Jahaliel. Wisdom dictates we learn how to hear the voice of God during the storm. This time God spoke through Jahaliel. Now it was up to the people to believe and act upon the word they received.

God heard and answered their prayers and the enemy was defeated. After the victory, they gathered in the valley of Berakah.

> 2 Chronicles 20:26
> *On the fourth day they assembled in the Valley*
> *of Berakah, where they praised the Lord. This is*
> *why it is called the Valley of Berakah to this day.*

Likewise, God honored our faith and prayers. In three years the school became debt-free, and we had our Berakah celebration. What a mighty God we serve.

This was one amazing journey, but it started with hearing the voice of God clearly.

Key #3 Learn to Hear the Voice of God for Yourself

- *KEY #4* -

STRANGE HAPPENINGS: GOD OR THE DEVIL?

There is a fierce debate taking place around the world regarding *strange happenings*. How do we know when something, even though strange, is of God or of the devil?

There are fakes, charlatans, and false prophets in many churches, but just because something is strange does not mean it is not from God or it is of God.

One national pastor held a conference in which he lambasted a certain Christian denomination saying that they were demon-led because of strange behavior.

Listening to this pastor, I became very concerned because accusing a church of being led by the devil when it's being led by God is blasphemy. With that in mind I decided to outline *a very strange church* I read about. Before listing this church, it's important to say I am not writing to defend the Cessation, Continuing, Armenian, Calvinist, or Charismatic theologies. I am simply writing in defense of the true Gospel contained in the Bible. I am also writing to try to keep people from being deceived. We are living in very serious times, and the body of Christ needs to know how to clearly discern between what God is doing and what God is not doing.

Here is the *strange* church I mentioned. *Please read this chapter in its entirety to get a full perspective.*

Strange Church?

1. People at this church were praying against storms and hurricanes.

2. They were praying to raise people from the dead.

3. The pastor even spit on a man's eyes to cure his blindness.

4. On one occasion the preacher spit on the ground and put the dirt on a man.

5. On another occasion the pastor spit on his fingers and touched the man's tongue. Many call this *the spitting church*.

6. One deacon took the preacher's handkerchief and sent it to his sick relatives. Women at the church were touching the pastor with their aprons and then sending them to their sick friends for healing.

7. At one meeting they were praying for demon possessed people as well as people with skin diseases. You name the disease, and they were praying for it.

8. The pastor and deacons are also speaking to the sun and cursing trees.

9. Tax time came and you would not believe what the pastor did. He sent one of his deacons to the lake to catch fish. He told him to open the fish mouth and he would find enough money to pay taxes for both of them.

I know many people would call this pastor a heretic and his followers deceived and following a false religion.

If you did, you would be calling Jesus and the disciple's heretics. I shudder writing that.

Let me give you more information on this strange church. Let us go through each point.

1. People at this church are praying against storms and hurricanes.

    Matthew 8:26 (NIV)
    He replied, You of little faith, why are you so afraid? Then he got up and rebuked the winds and the waves, and it was completely calm.

2. They were praying to raise people from the dead.

    Matthew 10:7–8 (NIV)
    As you go, proclaim this message: The kingdom of heaven has come near. Heal the sick, raise the dead, cleanse those who have leprosy, drive out demons. Freely you have received; freely give.

3. The pastor even spit on a man's eyes to cure his blindness.

    Mark 8:22–23
    They came to Bethsaida, and some people brought a blind man and begged Jesus to touch him. He took the blind man by the hand and led him outside the village. When he had spit on the man's eyes and put his hands on him, Jesus asked, "Do you see anything?"

4. On one occasion the preacher spit on the ground and put the dirt on the man.

John 9:6
After saying this, he spit on the ground, made some mud with the saliva, and put it on the man's eyes.

5. On another occasion the pastor spit on his fingers and touched the man's tongue.

    Mark 7:33
    After he took him aside, away from the crowd, Jesus put his fingers into the man's ears. Then he spit and touched the man's tongue.

6. One deacon took the preacher's handkerchief and sent to his sick relatives. Women at the church were touching the pastor with their aprons and then sending them to their sick friends for healing. *Acts 19:11–12, "God did extraordinary miracles through Paul, so that even handkerchiefs and aprons that had touched him were taken to the sick, and their illnesses were cured and the evil spirits left them."*

7. At one meeting they were praying for demon possessed people as well as people with skin diseases. Whatever the disease was, they were praying for it.

    Matthew 4:24 (NIV)
    News about him spread all over Syria, and people brought to him all who were ill with various diseases, those suffering severe pain, the demon-possessed, those having seizures, and the paralyzed; and he healed them.

8. The pastor and deacons are also speaking to the sun and cursing trees.

Joshua 10:12–13
On the day the Lord gave the Amorites over to Israel, Joshua said to the Lord in the presence of Israel: 'Sun, stand still over Gibeon, and you, moon, over the Valley of Aijalon.' So the sun stood still, and the moon stopped, till the nation avenged itself on its enemies.

Mark 11:14
Then he said to the tree, 'May no one ever eat fruit from you again.' And his disciples heard him say it.

9. Tax time came and you would not believe what the pastor did. He sent one of his deacons to the lake to catch fish. He told him to open the fish mouth and he would find enough money to pay taxes for both of them.

Matthew 17:27
But so that we may not cause offense, go to the lake and throw out your line. Take the first fish you catch; open its mouth and you will find a four-drachma coin. Take it and give it to them for my tax and yours.

There are many more *strange* stories in the Bible:

- A donkey *spoke* Numbers 22 (talk about *strange*):

- Samson was strong because he had long hair: Judges 16

- Elijah ran faster than a chariot: 1 Kings 18:46. (Not even Usain Bolt who is the world's fastest runner in recorded history could do this).

- Abraham and his wife Sarah had a son when he was 100 years old and Sarah was 90: Genesis 21.

- Three guys were thrown into a fiery furnace and did not burn: Daniel 3.

- Phillip disappeared and time traveled: Acts 8.

- Jonah lived in the belly of a fish for three days: Jonah 1:17.

- Methuselah lived to be 969 years old: Genesis 5:27.

- Peter walked on water: Matthew 14:22–31.

- David, only a youth, killed a lion and a bear with his bare hands: 1 Samuel 17:34–37.

- Some musicians blew their trumpets and shouted causing a protected wall surrounding a city to collapse: Joshua 6:20.

Here is the major one:

- Jesus was born of a virgin: Matthew 1:23.

The truth is, from start to finish, the Bible is full of *strange* happenings, stories that defy human logic. It takes serious faith to believe the *strange* stories listed. God's ways have always been unusual. As a matter of fact, that's the norm in Scripture.

I do not understand all the *strange* ways of God, but I accept the precious Word of God by faith, and I believe it from cover to cover. I also know many of my friends have subscribed to the view that the gifts of the Spirit ceased after the canonization process was complete. They submit 1 Corinthians 13:8–10 to support their theories.

> 1 Corinthians 13:8–10 (NIV)
> *Love never fails. But where there are prophecies,*

they will cease; where there are tongues, they will be stilled; where there is knowledge, it will pass away. For we know in part and we prophesy in part, but when completeness comes, what is in part disappears."

I totally disagree with my friends' conclusion because the Bible says nothing about canonization. The meaning of *perfect* is an open question. The Scripture also says that *knowledge* shall pass away. Knowledge has not passed away yet; it is still expanding. So how can we use that one verse to say the gifts have ceased?

The Scripture tells us to eagerly desire spiritual gifts.

> 1 Corinthians 14:1a
> *Follow the way of love and eagerly desire spiritual gifts."*

Another reason for my disagreement is, God gave us a blueprint for the *church*. He did not say the *early* church. He said *the church*. This blue print is found in 1 Corinthians 12:28, *"And in the church God has appointed first of all apostles, second prophets, third teachers, then workers of miracles, also those having gifts of healing, those able to help others, those with gifts of administration, and those speaking in different kinds of tongues."*

- Finally, the Scripture says in 1 Corinthians 14:39–40, *"Therefore, my brothers, be eager to prophesy, and do not forbid speaking in tongues. But everything should be done in a fitting and orderly way."*

With all those verses and more, how can a pastor just arbitrarily pull out one verse and tell the world the gifts in the book of Acts are finished? The question that needs an answer is, "What do you do when you encounter something strange?"

Here are my recommendations.

1. Pray and ask God to clearly show you if this is from Him or not. There are many fakes out there, and we need to be careful.

2. Check the Word. If it contradicts the Word, dismiss it. God will never contradict His Word.

3. Ask a few people you trust spiritually to pray with you for clarity.

4. God is not the author of confusion. Therefore if you find confusion, tread very carefully.

5. Search for any Biblical precedent for this strange happening.

6. Ask: "What is the result of this strange happening?"

7. Discern whether God is being glorified or man.

8. Ask: "Are people being drawn to Jesus?"

9. Do you observe lives being transformed?

10. Does this bear witness with your spirit? Jesus said that He is going to lead us by our spirit. Are you Spirit-led? If you are, how do you know? Are there different things you can look at in your life and say that was not me; I was being led by the Spirit? In chapter 18 I will go into more depth explaining what it means to walk by the spirit. If the spirit is leading you, in time God will reveal to you if this was from Him or not.

Key #4. Strange Happenings: God or the Devil?

- *KEY #5* -

DON'T TRUST YOURSELF

Proverbs 28:26
He who trusts in himself is a fool, but he who walks in wisdom is kept safe.

In chapter 1, we briefly addressed the subject of not trusting ourselves. I would like to expand more on this concept here.

In college, I had a friend who made a boast. He said you could follow him around with a video camera twenty-four hours a day, and you would not find any dirt. Sad to say, my friend had deceived himself.

There is no one who can honestly make that boast. We are all imperfect human beings prone to make mistakes. That is why as Christians we are grateful to God for His grace and mercy.

Sad to say, my friend is now divorced. When I asked him what happened, he said he had cheated on his wife. He was very disappointed and shocked. He kept saying that he did not know how this could have happened to him.

He had many questions, so we decided to get together for lunch. At our meeting, he sat broken-hearted and wanted to know my secret. He wanted to know what preserved me from making the same mistake. He said, "You are traveling all the time. You face a barrage of temptation. What has kept you?"

I was very happy to tell him.

My secret is found in *1 Corinthians 10:12, Wherefore let him that thinketh he standeth take heed lest he fall.*

If David, a man after God's own heart, could fall, who am I to deceive myself into believing that I am above temptation?

I have never cheated on my wife, and I don't plan to. At the same time, I know that anyone who puts themselves at the wrong place at the wrong time is playing with fire and begging for trouble. As a result, it is imperative that all of us put a system in place to protect ourselves.

My friend fell because he trusted himself. He fell because he put himself in a place where he thought he would be safe from temptation. He fell because he never thought he could fall. He fell because he did not have a plan of escape. He fell because he thought he could stand and fight.

There is no place in Scripture where we are told to stand and fight temptation. We are commanded to flee. *2 Timothy 2:22, "Flee the evil desires of youth and pursue righteousness, faith, love and peace, along with those who call on the Lord out of a pure heart."*

The Scripture also tells us to shun the very appearance of evil. *Proverbs 3:7, "Do not be wise in your own eyes; fear the Lord and shun evil."*

The Scripture is saying, "Don't trust yourself. It might not be evil, but if it looks like evil, shun it."

The lure and pull of evil is very strong. Men are visual while women are verbal. A man reacts to what he sees while women react to what they hear. A beautiful woman passes by and all men want to look. The way to handle this is not to deceive ourselves by pretending we are above temptation. The way to handle this is by applying Biblical mandate. *Flee.*

Learning how to handle temptation is one of the principles for guarding against deception. If you don't, you are bound to fail. As the motto goes, "Failure to plan is planning to fail."

It is not a matter of **if** you are going to be tempted, it's just **when**, *Ephesians 6:13, "Therefore put on the full armor of God, so that when the day of evil comes you may be able to stand your ground and after you have done everything to stand."*

The day of evil comes in many forms: temptation, tragedy, sickness—you name it. Since you know it is going to happen, what are you doing to prepare? Putting a plan into place is a major step in keeping you during the test. Let's take another test here.

The Bible says in *Psalm 119:11, "Thy word have I hid in mine heart that I might not sin against thee."*

Ask yourself a question: "Here comes temptation. What words have I hidden in my heart so I will not sin against God?"

Take the test right now and repeat out loud the words you have hidden in your heart that will keep you from falling. If none come to mind, here are a few to help. Start with this motto: **Failure is not an option.**

Second, memorize and hide these verses in your heart. *James 4:7, "Submit yourselves then to God. Resist the devil and he will flee from you."* Note the verse does not only say "resist the devil and he will flee." It gives us a clear plan of action:

1.   Submit. (Submit means to turn my will completely over

2. Resist. (This means a fight is taking place. You cannot resist if you are not fully submitted to God.)

3. The devil flees. (I have victory because I submitted and resisted.)

> James 1:12
> *Blessed is the man who perseveres under trial, because when he has stood the test, he will receive the crown of life that God has promised to those who love him.*

> 1 Corinthians 10:13
> *There hath no temptation taken you but such as is common to man: but God is faithful, who will not suffer you to be tempted above that ye are able; but will with the temptation also make a way to escape, that ye may be able to bear it.*

God will make a way of escape; look for that way and take it.

> I Corinthians 6:18–20
> *Flee from sexual immorality. All other sins a man commits are outside his body, but he who sins sexually sins against his own body. Do you not know that your body is a temple of the Holy Spirit, who is in you whom you have received from God? You are not your own. You were bought with a price. Therefore honor God with your body.*

> Romans 12:1
> *Therefore I urge you brothers in view of God's mercy to offer your bodies as living sacrifices holy and pleasing to God—this is your spiritual act of worship.*

2 Corinthians 10:5
We demolish arguments and every pretension that sets itself up against the knowledge of God, and we take captive every thought to make it obedient to Christ.

This passage commands us to take captive every thought. Cultivate the habit of taking thoughts captive to Christ, and that in itself will help to keep you from falling.

We have all heard the saying, "A bird can fly over your head, but it does not have to build a nest." One friend jokingly said, "I know that, but why does the bird have to fly so often?" Thoughts can come into your mind, but by taking them captive, you will have victory. The flesh is the biggest enemy you have—not the devil. The devil will put thoughts and ideas in your mind, but you are the one who determines what course of action to take.

Key #5 Don't Trust Yourself

- *KEY #6* -

DO NOT CONDEMN
A FALLEN BELIEVER

A few years ago, a famous minister fell. Another prominent pastor was asked to comment, and I will never forget his unfortunate words.

He said, "This is a cancer in the church, and it needs to be rooted out." I was shocked and said to myself, "I don't remember reading that in the Bible." I read *Galatians 6:1, "Brothers and sisters, if someone is caught in a sin, you who live by the Spirit should restore that person gently. But watch yourselves, or you also may be tempted."*

This second pastor also fell and has never fully recovered from that fall. He was facing the same problems that the other pastor he had condemned was facing. In an interview he was asked, "If you knew you had this problem, why didn't you tell someone?"

He said, "Who?" I was shocked that this pastor had no one he thought trustworthy enough to confide in.

If pastors are struggling finding someone to confide in, I know the general public is going through the same struggle. Even though it is difficult to find trustworthy people, you must make it a top priority in your life. We all need accountability partners.

Without accountability, you risk the danger of falling. Make sure you have people in your life who will hold you accountable by praying for you and asking you the tough questions. These people must be trustworthy because if trust is broken, your friend won't be truthful when asked the tough questions.

Make sure that what is said at the accountability sessions stays there.

Don't be afraid to confront your friend, either. If he is a real friend, he will protect you.

> Proverbs 17:9
> *He who covers over an offense promotes love,*
> *but whoever repeats the matter separates close*
> *friends.*

The danger many have faced is the fear that if they confront someone in sin, they are condemning them. That's far from the truth. If you truly love someone, you would never condemn them, but you would confront them.

Don't make it easy for your friends to sin or feel good about their sin. At the same time, don't condemn them. There is a healthy balance to be achieved here.

All Christians have a built in alarm system. He is called the Holy Spirit. When the alarm goes off, we need to take heed. A friend called me one day to confess his sins and to explain how terrible he felt. I told him to give God thanks that he felt terrible. **The day we sin and do not feel bad about our sin should be a scary day.**

This means we have become desensitized to the promptings of the Holy Spirit, and that's a dangerous place to be.

Ask the tough questions.

Do not say, "It's none of my business." Ask God to give you the wisdom for *when* to confront, *how* to confront, and *where* to confront. Love the person enough to confront them—not condemn them.

Key #6 Do Not Condemn A Fallen Believer

Trust Is Earned

One debate that has taken place for years is the question, "Is trust given or earned?" I believe trust is earned. Trust can be broken, but I believe once a foundation of trust is established, your friendship can last forever.

Do not use blind trust—it is a recipe for deception. Many have used blind trust to believe their friends and religious leaders. I can't stress how dangerous this is.

The sad part about this key is that many times you do not know if you can trust someone until trouble starts. In a war, when a soldier says, "I've got your back," this means you can forge ahead without looking back. You move forward because you trust the person walking behind you. The same is also true for pilots in war who trust their *wing men.*

In basketball there is a pass called a *no-look pass.* This pass is only attempted once a foundation of trust has been established. Without looking, the player passes the ball to a spot because he knows the player he trusts will be there.

If you were in trouble and could only make one phone call, who would you call? Who would you trust that all things being equal, you know that person would answer their phone and also have ideas on how to navigate the crisis?

I am sure the person you would call has proven themselves to be trustworthy, or you would not make the call.

I have met people who became disillusioned because they discovered they were living a lie for many years and did not know it. They gave another person blind trust, which the other person used to deceive them. Sad to say, a few have paid with their lives.

Can I trust you to confess my faults?

Be very careful to whom you confess your faults.

You might be surprised that what you told someone in private is now being broadcast publicly. The devil has been fighting a long time, and he knows how to be patient. He will wait patiently until you are really hurting and in a vulnerable place to use people to hurt you. He will also use so-called friends to do the greatest damage. You really don't know who your lifetime friends are until your friendship gets tested. Many times you don't know what's in someone until they get squeezed. During the heat of the battle, people's true characters are revealed. Sad to say, but that's when the devil does his greatest work.

As the saying goes, you cannot stop people from hurting you, but you do not have to give them the information to do so. **Can someone trust you to keep private information private?**

> Proverbs 17:9
> *He who covers over an offense promotes love,*
> *but whoever repeats the matter separates close*
> *friends.*

Can your friends trust you to tell them the truth no matter how much it hurts?

Proverbs 27:6
Wounds from a friend can be trusted, but an enemy multiplies kisses.

Have you earned the right to be heard?

Make sure you have a record of supporting the person so when the time comes to correct them by being brutally honest, they will accept your criticism. Once they know your motives are pure, you have earned the right to speak into their lives.

Can your friends trust you to be there to help them in their darkest hour?

Can they trust your prayer life? If they are in trouble and you promise to pray for them, will you fulfill that promise?

Can they trust you to go hungry on their behalf? Will you fast and pray for them?

Trust is one of the key principles in guarding against deception. Once a foundation of trust is established, that will help to keep you from being deceived. Remember, trust is earned.

Key #7 Trust Is Earned

WISDOM

Do you want something more valuable than silver and gold?

Do you want to be blessed?

Do you want a long life?

If you do, search for wisdom. One of the main keys to guarding against deception is wisdom.

> Proverbs 3:13–16
> *Blessed are those who find wisdom, those who gain understanding, for she is more profitable than silver and yields better returns than gold. She is more precious than rubies; nothing you desire can compare with her. Long life is in her right hand; in her left hand are riches and honor.*

Once a foundation of wisdom is established, you have one of the key ingredients to guard against deception. Do you have wisdom from the:

Tongue?

No. Mind?

No. Spirit? Yes.

The tongue is simply a member of the body. It has no power of its own unless you give it power.

The mind is the filtering station. It processes tons of information, and then your spirit tells you what to say. Make sure you weigh your words carefully.

It's also important to understand the difference between *knowledge* and *wisdom*. Knowledge pertains to the acquisition of information. Wisdom refers to the processing and application of information.

To state it another way, "Knowledge is knowing the right thing to do, but wisdom is doing it."

Getting wisdom should be one of our primary goals in life.

> Proverbs 4:7
> *Wisdom is the principal thing; therefore get wisdom: and with all thy getting, get understanding.*
>
> Ecclesiastes 7:19
> *Wisdom makes one wise person more powerful than ten rulers in a city.*

Saying wisdom is the principal thing means it is the most important thing. It is what we consult to make our decisions and draw our conclusions.

Principal, as an adjective, means "first in order of importance." As a noun, it means "the person with the highest authority or most important position in an organization, institution, or group."

In your life, wisdom needs to be one of your top priorities.

- Wisdom will teach you how to guard against deception.

- Wisdom will preserve your life.

- Wisdom will show you the correct path to take.

- Wisdom will help you to discern the voice of God and also to know through whom God is speaking.

- Wisdom has a beginning. It starts with the fear of the Lord.

> Proverbs 9:10
> *The fear of the Lord is the beginning of wisdom, and knowledge of the Holy One is understanding.*

What does it really mean to fear God?

For a long time, I wrestled with that question. One day I discovered a formula that answered this question.

Many people say the Bible is not a book of formulas, but I beg to disagree. Formulas are all over the Bible.

What is a formula?

A *formula* is described as a system used to achieve a particular goal. Here is one I discovered.

DNC+T+R=Knowing God's will.

I found this formula in Romans 12:2 which says, *"Do not conform any longer to the pattern of this world, but be transformed by the renewing of your mind. Then you will be able to test and approve what God's will is–His good, pleasing and perfect will."*

To know God's will:

DNC—Do not conform to the pattern of this world. To *conform* means to abandon one's belief system regarding certain issues and acquiesce to the demand of one's culture. There are issues that are becoming cultural norms, and God is saying, "Do not conform to these new belief systems." We have to say no.

T—Transformed. Be transformed. *Transformation* means something radical has taken place. We have changed.

R—Renew. Our minds are renewed because transformation took place.

Renewing means going back to the true original. "Re" is a prefix meaning, "going back" to something. Words like "repent," "restore," "refurbish," and "renew" all mean going back to something.

God is telling us to renew our minds by following His words carefully.

That is why Proverbs 3:5 says, *"Trust in the Lord with all your heart and lean not on your own understanding."*

Our way of understanding things has been contaminated by the world's thinking. It is imperative that we have a total mind transformation in order to understand God's will.

God's will is that we fear Him.

In addressing the question, "What does it mean to fear the Lord?" the formula is found in *Proverbs 2:1–5:*

> *My son, if you accept my words and store up my commands within you, turning your ear to wisdom and applying your heart to understanding–indeed, if you call out for insight*

and cry aloud for understanding, and if you look for it as for silver and search for it as for hidden treasure, then you will understand the fear of the Lord and find the knowledge of God.

Let's go back and unpack those verses. To understand the fear of the Lord, we must:

• Accept God's Word.

• Store His commands in our hearts.

• Turn our ears to wisdom.

• Apply our hearts to understanding.

• Call out for insight.

• Cry aloud for understanding.

• Search for wisdom just like a hunter searches for hidden treasure.

If we do all the above, we will understand what it means to fear the Lord. There are also benefits attached to fearing God.

Psalm 33:1
But the eyes of the Lord are on those who fear him, on those whose hope is in his unfailing love.

The eyes of the Lord are on whom? Those who fear Him. How do you know you fear God? What is the proof?

Psalm 34:7
The angel of the Lord encamps around those who fear him, and he delivers them.

The angel of the Lord encamps around whom? Those who fear Him. How do you know you fear God?

Proverbs 8:13
To fear the Lord is to hate evil; I hate pride and arrogance, evil behavior and perverse speech.

Do you hate evil? If you truly fear God, you would hate evil.

To fear God does not mean you walk around all day trembling in fear that He is going to zap you. To fear God means you have a holy reverence for Him. This means you will not violate the principles He has outlined for your life.

Principles govern everything. If the governing principles are violated by our failure to fear, we are to be blamed for the consequences of our decisions—not God.

A stove is a good thing, and I love my stove, but I also fear my stove. If I do not fear my stove and deceive myself into believing that the laws that govern heat do not apply to me, after one touch I will discover the extent of my deception.

At home we have a saying when it comes to handling a dangerous object: *respect it.*

If you do not respect dangerous objects, very soon you will hurt yourself. The object is not the problem. The problem rests with our inability to respect the dangerous object.

We love our children and our children love us, even though they fear us. They know that if they violate the rules, consequences follow. Even so, they are fully persuaded of our love for them.

We find the same is true with God. I know He loves me, and I love Him, too. At the same time I know that if I violate His principles, He will forgive me. But I still have to deal with the consequences of my disobedience.

So how do I get wisdom to guard against deception?

Ask God as *James 1:5–8 says, "If any of you lacks wisdom, you should ask God, who gives generously to all without finding fault, and it will be given to you. But when you ask, you must believe and not doubt, because the one who doubts is like a wave of the sea, blown and tossed by the wind. That person should not expect to receive anything from the Lord. Such a person is double-minded and unstable in all they do."*

To receive wisdom from God, we need to know the conditions, because receiving wisdom from God is conditional. The conditions are outlined in James 1:5–8:

- Ask

- Believe

- Get rid of doubt

- Do not be double-minded

Apply these conditions to your life and God guarantees that you will possess wisdom.

Key #8 Wisdom

LOVE

Pop singer Tina Turner raised a question in her famous song, "What's Love Got to Do with It?"

I would like to pose the same question in regards to deception. What's love got to do with guarding against deception?

Everything.

If we do not know what true love really is, we will deceive ourselves into believing that there is true love, when in reality true love is absent.

What does it really mean to love someone?

Over the years we have all heard people say, "I really thought he or she loved me. They said all the right words, but later on I discovered I was deceived. It was a ruse to trick me."

So what does it *really* mean to love someone? We need to take our cue from God.

> John 3:16
> *For God so loved the world that he gave his only begotten Son, that whosoever believeth in him should not perish, but have everlasting life.*

God loved us so much He did something.

What did He do?

He sent His only son Jesus to die for us.

> John 15:13
> *Greater love hath no man than this, that a man
> lay down his life for his friends.*

Many times, people are deceived because they believe that just because someone tells them that they love them, they do. That's a recipe for deception.

There are nations in the world where men say they love their wives, yet they beat and abuse them. This is one of the biggest lies the devil can tell anyone. You cannot say you love your wife and beat and abuse her. If you do, you are deceived and need to repent. Desist and get counseling right away.

Many times in premarital counseling, I ask the couple one question: *What does it really mean to love the other person?*

Over the years I have been given many different answers. To truly understand love, I encourage the couples to filter their definition of love through 1 Corinthians 13.

> 1 Corinthians 13:4–7
> *Love is patient, love is kind. It does not envy, it
> does not boast, it is not proud. It does not
> dishonor others, it is not self-seeking, it is not
> easily angered, it keeps no record of wrongs.
> Love does not delight in evil but rejoices with
> the truth. It always protects, always trusts,
> always hopes, always perseveres.*

Let's take a second look at this passage and pause after each point to ask the appropriate question. In a counseling session, after asking each question, I would ask the other spouse if they believe the person fits the description in the verse.

Love is patient.

Husband (Are you patient?) . . .

Wife (Do you think your husband is patient?) . . .

Love is kind.

Husband (Are you kind?) . . .

Wife (Do you think your husband is kind?) . . .

It does not envy.

Husband (Do you envy?) . . .

Wife (Do you think your husband envies?) . . .

It does not boast.

Husband (Do you boast?) . . .

Wife (Do you think your husband boasts?) . . .

It is not proud.

Husband (Are you proud?) . . .

Wife (Do you think your husband is proud?) . . .

It does not dishonor others.

Husband (Do you dishonor others?) . . .

Wife (Do you think your husband dishonors others?) . . .

It is not self-seeking.

Husband (Are you self-seeking?) . . .

Wife (Do you think your husband is self-seeking?) . . .

It is not easily angered.

Husband (Do you become angry easily?) . . .

Wife (Does your husband become angry easily?) . . .

It keeps no record of wrongs.

Husband (Do you keep a record of wrongs?) . . .

Wife (Does your husband keeps a record of wrongs?) . . .

Love does not delight in evil, but rejoices with the truth.

Husband (Do you delight in evil or in the truth?) . . .

Wife (Does your husband delight in evil or in the truth?) . . .

It always protects.

Husband (Do you always protect?) . . .

Wife (Do you feel protected?) . . .

Always trusts.

Husband (Do you always trust?) . . .

Wife (Do you think your husband always trusts?) . . .

Always hopes.

Husband (Do you always hope?) . . .

Wife (Does your husband always hope?) . . .

Always perseveres.

Husband (Do you persevere?) . . .

Wife (Does your husband persevere?) . . .

Now reverse the exercise and do it again with the wife asking the same questions.

After taking the 1 Corinthians love test, I am sure everyone will agree that we all have work to do when it comes to fulfilling the Biblical definition of love. When someone says he or she loves you, don't deceive yourself by just accepting their words. Filter their *words* and *actions* through 1 Corinthians 13.

The people Jesus told to depart from Him in Matthew 7:21 thought they knew and loved Him, but Jesus basically said, "Who are you?" The question is often asked. If you were on trial for loving God, would there be enough evidence to convict you?

Here is what the Scripture says about the people who love God:

> John 14:15
> *If you love me, you will obey what I command.*

Do you obey God's commands?

> John 14:21
> *Whoever has my commands and obeys them, he is the one who loves me.*

John 4:20
If anyone says, 'I love God,' yet hates his brother, he is a liar. For anyone who does not love his brother, whom he has seen, cannot love God, whom he has not seen.

Psalm 91:14–16
Because he loves me I will rescue him; I will protect him, for he acknowledges my name. He will call upon me, and I will answer him; I will be with him in trouble, I will deliver him and honor him. With long life will I satisfy him and show him my salvation.

In one of my devotion times, I felt the Lord say this about the people who truly love Him:

"They bug Me, they hound Me; they tell Me how much they love Me. They buy Me gifts and spend time with Me. They can't go anywhere without bragging about Me. In every situation that comes along, they find a way to bring Me into the subject.

"I am the first person they talk to in the morning and the last one they talk to at night. They dream about Me, paint pictures of Me; write songs about Me. Some even set up a special room where they read My love letters to them and worship Me.

"People say they talk too much about Me, but they say they can't help it because they are in love with Me.

"Many have been tortured, imprisoned, and humiliated just because they love Me. Others have given their lives.

"I know they love Me because I have heard their words, seen their hearts, thoughts, and actions. Their rhetoric and their actions match, and that pleases Me.

"Because of this, I will deliver them. When they call I will answer. When trouble comes, I will be with them and will deliver them. I am going to command My angels to guard them, and I will bless them and give them a long life."

Understanding the principles of love is a key ingredient in laying a foundation to guard against deception.

Key #9 Love

Know Who You Are

Who are you?

I am not talking about what you do for a living or your reputation. I am talking about your identity—the real you. Many people have deceived themselves by believing their public image. They base their identity on their reputation and what they do for a living. This inevitably leads to deception.

There is a saying: "Show me your friends and I will tell you who you are." There is some truth to that saying, but not 100 percent. You can hang out with the wrong friends and one day wake up to realize they are quite different from you.

Years ago, one of my barbers went to prison. He told me one morning he woke up, looked around him, and said, "I am not one of these guys."

This revelation changed his life, and today he is a different person operating a very successful barber shop.

So who are you? Have you clearly defined yourself?

Many are deceived because they allow their reputation or friends to define their identity. Reputation is not the real you. Your reputation is what you are known for or what others think of you. Your true identity is found when there is no one around, and it's just you and God. Who are you then?

Here are a few of the things I do. I am a Christian concert pianist, a pastor, an arranger, a producer, an agent, a teacher, a counselor, an author, a basketball coach, a martial-artist. Not to mention that I am a husband and father to our four daughters. From that list, who am I?

Many will say a Christian concert pianist, but that is not who I am—that is what I do. (Notice I put *Christian* first before a pianist.)

I did that purposely because many process their identity through their career and their skin color. I do not. In the future we won't be asked what we did for a living or what color we were. We will be asked if we knew Jesus and accepted Him as Lord and Savior.

If you don't know who you are, someone or something will define you.

Having another person or your place of employment define you is very dangerous. What will happen if they change their definition or if you change jobs? Who are you then?

Keep in mind that people's perspective or perception of you could be right or wrong. We need wisdom to know the difference, and that can only be accomplished by being totally honest with ourselves. We will cover this with an honesty test in chapter 24. We can be deceived by others, but when we deceive ourselves by believing our public image, that's when it gets really dangerous.

When you think of yourself, what do you think?

Here are two sobering reminders.

Romans 12:3
For by the grace given me I say to every one of you: Do not think of yourself more highly than you ought, but rather think of yourself with sober judgment, in accordance with the measure of faith God has given you."

Galatians 6:3
For if a man think himself to be something, when he is nothing, he deceiveth himself.

Deceived people think of themselves more highly than they ought. They base their identity on their reputation, and when reality sets in, they get disillusioned. Don't get me wrong. Reputation is important, but identity has to come before reputation.

The Scripture says in *Proverbs 23:7, "For as he thinketh in his heart, so is he."*

Focus on your heart. Internally what do you think of yourself? The Bible says that out of the abundance of the heart the mouth speaks.

What's the condition of your heart? What are the thoughts in your heart?

Luke 6:45 ESV
The good person out of the good treasure of his heart produces good, and the evil person out of his evil treasure produces evil, for out of the abundance of the heart his mouth speaks."

So who are you? You are a three-part being: body, soul, and spirit.

Your *body* is basically a disposable suit. You need it to function on the earth. Once you die, it decomposes and is gone forever.

Your *soul* consists of your mind, your will, and your emotions.

Your *spirit* is the real you. That is who you are—a spirit being created by God to accomplish great works for Him.

You also need to know the difference between *reputation* and *character*. **Reputation is who others think you are. Character is who you are when no one is looking.**

There is a very important saying: **Make sure you have character over talent because your talent will take you places where your character cannot sustain you.**

One famous athlete discovered this the hard way. He had talent, and this talent took him to the top of his sport. Very soon, his character was challenged, and he got caught cheating on his wife. During his press conference he said, "I felt I was entitled to this." He felt because of his stature (reputation) he could do anything and get away with it. Sad to say, very soon reality set in, and he discovered he was deceived. This deception cost him his marriage, his reputation, and millions of dollars. It will take years to repair the damage he has done to his reputation.

So what's your reputation?

Do not deceive yourself into thinking that you do not need a good reputation—you do!

Do you have a good name?

> Proverbs 22:1
> *A good name is rather to be chosen than great riches, and loving favor rather than silver and gold.*

So who are you, apart from a spirit being? You are a child of God created by God to do good works for His kingdom. If you are a Christian:

- You are born again (I Peter 1:23).

- You are a new creation (2 Corinthians 5:17).

- You are a dwelling for the Holy Spirit (Ephesians 2:22).

- You are chosen and dearly loved (Colossians 3:12).

- You are more than a conqueror (Romans 8:37).

- You are the righteousness of God (2 Corinthians 5:21).

- You are a part of God's kingdom (Revelation 1:6).

- You are no longer condemned (Romans 8:1-2).

In processing your true identity, make a vow to erase from your vocabulary statements like, "I am a failure; I cannot do anything right; I am a loser;" and so on. Get rid of those sayings. Yes, you might have made some mistakes. We have all made mistakes, but you should never process your identity through your mistakes. You are not a failure. Failure is an event, not a person. You are one of a kind, and God knew what He was doing when He created you. Just keep saying what the psalmist said in *Psalm 139:14, "I praise you because I am fearfully and wonderfully made; your works are wonderful, I know that full well."*

Key #10 Know Who You Are

Keys For Living
PART TWO

- *KEY #11* -

PERSEVERANCE

Perseverance is a word that suggests difficulties, storms, challenges, and obstacles that need to be overcome. What does perseverance really mean?

Noun: *Steadfastness in doing something despite difficulty or delay in achieving success.*

Synonyms: *Persistence, tenacity, determination, staying power, indefatigability, steadfastness.*

Perseverance is an invaluable key that everyone needs for success in life. Invaluable means something is so important that you cannot do without it.

- No gas in your car—you will not get very far.

- No food—you will die of hunger.

- No water—you will die of thirst.

- No faith—you cannot please God.

    Hebrews 11:6
    And without faith it is impossible to please God, because anyone who comes to him must believe that he exists and that he rewards those who earnestly seek him.

69

While writing this book, I discovered the true meaning of perseverance.

I was coaching a basketball game, and during the game, the ball got stuck on the rim. Trying to help, I jumped to knock the ball loose. I cannot clearly explain what happened next, but what I vividly remember was hearing a pop and not getting very far in the air.

When I landed, I discovered I could not stand up. I grabbed my knees and realized my knee caps were in the wrong place. I fell to the floor and told the referees to call 911. The ambulance arrived and took me to the hospital where they told me I had dislocated both knees.

I told the doctor I had a concert in California, and I needed to get there. I hate missing concerts, so unless something is clearly out of my control, I will be there.

The doctor gave me two braces and pain medication and told me to contact the orthopedic surgeon when I returned.

I flew to California and played the concert. With the warm greetings from the folks in California and the pain medication, we had a great evening.

Following the concert, I took the red-eye flight back to Chicago. It was quite an eventful twenty-four hours.

On Monday, I visited the orthopedic surgeon. He examined my knees, looked at the x-rays, and then turned to me with a puzzled look on his face.

He said, "You went to California in this condition?" I confirmed I had, and he repeated the question with a look of shock and total disbelief. He then told me to wait and he left the room. He soon returned with another doctor and asked me to confirm that I had traveled to California in this condition. They both looked at me with disbelief and tried to figure out how this was even possible. Finally convinced that I was telling the truth, they gave me the bad news. I had torn both my quadriceps muscles and needed surgery as quickly as possible. They said that going to California was an amazing feat—one for the record books.

I then asked about the possibility of flying to Florida for my next concert. They said no. I pleaded, but they said this was a matter of life and death. With that, we had to cancel all out-of-state engagements.

I now had lots of time to think and ask many questions. One question I never asked was, "Why me?" I did not ask that question because I know times of testing will come to every family. It's not *if* a time of testing will come. It's just *when* and *in what form.*

> Ephesians 6:13
> *Therefore, put on the full armor of God, so that when the day of evil comes, you may be able to stand your ground, and after you have done everything, to stand.*

Since you know the day of testing will come, what are you going to do? What are your plans for dealing with times of testing?

I decided in advance that I needed to get to know God for myself. Once I did, I discovered that Romans 8:28 is a verse I could hold onto during times of testing. *Romans 8:28, "And we know that all things work together for good to them that love God, to them who are the called according to his purpose."*

That verse says *all things.* What does *all* mean? It means *everything.* The verse is not applicable to everyone. It qualifies the people who are affected—those who love God. Do you love God? How do you know that you love God?

In chapter 9 we covered what it means to really love God. In order to guard against deception, I have designed a checklist system that I use to help me navigate through my trials.

If my checklist comes up negative, then I rely on the first and last points.

CHECKLIST

1. God is sovereign. (This means I might not get an answer.)

2. Is there any sin in my life that could have led to this trial?

3. Did I take communion in an unworthy manner?

4. Depending on the situation, am I eating right and getting enough rest?

5. Is this an attack by the devil? If it is, how do I know?

6. Is this just an unfortunate accident?

7. God is sovereign.

Why is *knowing* important? It's important because deception can creep in if we are not careful. It's also important because my response to each point has to be different:

*   If it is sin, I need to repent.

*   If it is a lack of sleep and nutrition, I need to make sure I get enough sleep and eat the right foods.

*   If it is an attack by the devil, then I go into spiritual

warfare. Ephesians 6:10–18 and James 4:7 cover spiritual warfare.

- If it is an unfortunate accident, accept it for what it is and ask God to help you through. You do not need to apply spiritual warfare keys to an unfortunate accident.

So what do I believe happened in my accident?

I am not sure yet, but God used the situation for His glory. I know God will not hurt me to teach me a lesson. He will allow me to go through difficult things, which He will use for His glory. At the same time, I do not see God planning to send difficulty into my life to teach me a lesson when I am living right and have done nothing wrong. I am sure a few people might disagree here and say, "How about Job?" I will cover this question in chapter 14.

Five days after my knee surgery, my family had another situation that I am convinced was an attack by the devil.

My wife and children were in a store. Out of the clear blue, an older gentleman came over to them and started singing, "Some glad morning when this life is over, I'll fly away."

He then told them a story of being into witchcraft when he was younger. My wife then left that store and on the way, a vehicle turned in front of her. Trying to avoid this car, she swerved and hit a snow bank, which launched our van into the air.

With the van airborne, my wife heard our daughter Natasha scream, *"We are covered under the blood of Jesus."*

Miraculously, God rescued them, and the van landed on all four wheels with everyone safe.

First, we thought the vehicle was okay, but after encouragement from a few friends to have a mechanic examine it, we discovered it had sustained thousands of dollars in damage. You can always replace a vehicle, but you cannot replace your family. Praise God for His protection!

The lady who caused the incident said it was like a scene in the movies when a car is launched in midair. When the van went airborne, she thought it was going to flip. She was amazed it landed with no one hurt. Psalm 91 was definitely in operation, and we give God thanks for sending His angels to protect my family and to dismantle the plans of the evil one.

Following this, I asked myself a question. "What are the chances of a total stranger going up to my family, singing a song about death, talking about witchcraft, and then my wife having an accident?" I drew the conclusion that this was an attack by the devil.

With me being incapacitated, I felt the devil was trying to destroy my family. He failed!

During this journey, I asked God what He wanted to teach me from my knee accident.

He led me to James 1:2–4:

> *Consider it pure joy, my brothers and sisters, whenever you face trials of many kinds, because you know that the testing of your faith produces perseverance. Let perseverance finish its work so that you may be mature and complete, not lacking anything.*

I read, reread, and meditated on the verses and then got revelation.

I persevered through a major injury and got to California, a four-and-a-half hour flight from Chicago. Now God wants me to persevere so I can be a mature Christian. Dealing with a situation like this raises many questions, and if we are not careful, we can deceive ourselves by subscribing to one conclusion when the real reason is a totally different conclusion. No matter the situation, as long as you know you heard from God, persevere.

Trials produce perseverance. Allowing perseverance to complete its work leads to maturity and completion. God wants mature Christians, and He will use every situation in our lives to accomplish that.

Our responsibility is to really seek Him on His terms, walk in full obedience, and allow perseverance to have its perfect work.

Key #11 Perseverance

Understand Discipline and Suffering

Discipline and suffering are two words we all like to leave out of our vocabulary, but they are necessary words for us to include from a Biblical perspective if we are going to avoid deception.

There are times in our journey when God disciplines us, and there are times when we will suffer. We need wisdom to navigate both journeys.

> Hebrews 12:5–6
> *And have you completely forgotten this word of encouragement that addresses you as a father addresses his son? It says, My son, do not make light of the Lord's discipline, and do not lose heart when he rebukes you, because the Lord disciplines the one he loves, and he chastens everyone he accepts as his son.*

What does God's discipline look like? Discipline at times means punishment; an uncomfortable situation that no one likes. How do we know when God is disciplining us?

> Hebrews 12:7–8
> *Endure hardship as discipline; God is treating you as his children. For what children are not disciplined by their father? If you are not*

disciplined and everyone undergoes discipline then you are not legitimate, not true sons and daughters at all.

The verse says everyone undergoes discipline. That happens because we are all imperfect human beings who are prone to make mistakes. Discipline does not only refers to punishment. It can also mean correction. We could be heading in the wrong direction, and God needs to correct us. On the other hand, it could mean we are being disciplined because of sin.

David encountered God's discipline.

Psalm 38:1–3
Lord, do not rebuke me in your anger or discipline me in your wrath. Your arrows have pierced me, and your hand has come down on me. Because of your wrath there is no health in my body; there is no soundness in my bones because of my sin.

This psalm is a petition of David asking God not to discipline him in His wrath. David knew he was being punished by God because of his sin. Praise God for His grace today.

Many times discipline leads to suffering, and the Scripture says we glory in our suffering.

Romans 5:3–5
Not only so, but we also glory in our sufferings, because we know that suffering produces perseverance; And hope does not put us to shame, because God's love has been poured out into our hearts through the Holy Spirit, who has been given to us.

This verse is not an easy verse to digest. It says to glory in your suffering. How do you do that? It starts with understanding Biblical suffering. Not all suffering passes the Biblical test.

> 1 Peter 4:15–16
> *If you suffer, it should not be as a murderer or thief or any other kind of criminal, or even as a meddler. However, if you suffer as a Christian, do not be ashamed, but praise God that you bear that name.*

In order to truly comprehend suffering and discipline, we need to understand that discipline many times is applied to the disobedient. At the same time, suffering is *guaranteed* if you are a true follower of Christ. It is a natural byproduct whether we are walking in obedience or not. All Christians will suffer.

I would never discipline my children for doing the right thing. God won't discipline us for doing the right thing either, but we will all suffer for representing Christ.

Looking through the entire Bible, we see God never afflicts His righteous people with disease. He allows affliction for many different reasons, and the majority of the time it is because of disobedience.

It is very important to note, however, that satan will attack us even if we are walking in complete obedience to God's Word. Praise God, Jesus came to show us how we should respond. He responded to satan with the Word, and we need to do the same.

How do we know when an attack is from satan? How do we know when God is disciplining us? We know by staying close to God. He will reveal it to us.

Suffering can be a great teacher, and in that valley we can learn some powerful lessons. Every Christian will suffer, but when suffering is the issue, we have to make a distinction as to who the author of the suffering is so we can know how to respond.

If we say suffering is from God, there is nothing we can do about it but go through the process and wait.

God knows we will all suffer, but He uses it as He does everything for His glory. **Trials in and of themselves do not bring us to maturity. It is how we handle trials that we grow and mature.**

The question we need to address is, Who is the author of sickness?

This book is not a theological discourse on sickness and healing, but it is important to make a note here. The ministry of Jesus was a healing ministry—not one of hurting people. I could not see God desiring people to be sick and Jesus going against His will and heal them. If it is God's will for a person to be sick and that person goes to a doctor to get relief, that person would be fighting against God.

If that person then asks the church to pray for healing about a sickness they believe God wants them to have, that church would be praying against God's will, too.

Over the years I have heard people say, "Look at this person or that person. They love the Lord, and they have been sick for years." They then draw the conclusion that God does not heal today because of the person they hold up as the example. I can't stress how dangerous this line of thinking is. This line of reasoning basically tries to relegate God to human experience.

A few years ago I felt the Lord put this on my heart: **Never judge the Word through your circumstances. Always judge your circumstances through the Word.**

I have fought various ailments over the years. Whether I got healed or not is irrelevant. It does not matter who gets healed or who does not get healed. No one should use me or any other person as the standard for whether God heals or not. The only standard one should use is the Word of God.

The Word trumps everything. My experience, your experience, the experience of the people we see on TV should not be the litmus test. We need to ask one question: What does God's Word say regarding healing?

Many have quoted Paul's *thorn in the flesh* in 2 Corinthians 12:7. The problem I see with using that story is multifaceted.

1.   No one knows what the thorn in the flesh was. Many speculate it was an eye problem. The truth is, the Scripture does not tell us what the thorn was.

2.   No one knows if Paul died with this thorn. God used Paul to heal many people, so I would imagine the possibility of Paul being healed from this malady was very high.

3.   Others have said the thorn could have been a demon that followed Paul everywhere he went creating trouble for him. I could be wrong, but I feel this could be the correct interpretation of this passage. Ask yourself this question, "What is a messenger of Satan?"

The Greek word that is used here is *agellos,* which means *angel* or *messenger.* This was not just any messenger. This was a messenger of Satan—not a messenger of God. This suggests to me that a demonic force was sent against Paul.

Paul was able to go through this trial because he had heard from God. Whatever trials we face, we need to hear from God, too. God answered Paul by saying, "My grace is sufficient for you."

I am sure that is not what Paul wanted to hear. However, the good news was that he heard from God.

What is difficult for all of us is when we find ourselves going through a crisis, and God seems to be silent.

When God seems silent we just have to trust Him by faith knowing He is going to work out *whatever* the challenge is for His glory. Even if we are suffering or being disciplined by Him, as long as we love Him and have a personal relationship with Him, everything will work together for our good.

> Romans 8:28
> *And we know that all things work together for good to them that love God, to them who are the called according to his purpose."*

Key #12 Understand Discipline and Suffering

- Key #13 -

WHO IS THE AUTHOR OF SICKNESS?

Who is the author of sickness and disease? Is it God, the devil, or simply a natural byproduct of living in a fallen world?

We really need to pray for discernment on this issue because many people have been deceived believing God is the one who wanted them sick, when the truth is, the devil is the one trying to kill them.

I have read where many people say God is in charge and as a result He is the one ultimately responsible for everything. Others have said it is the devil. Still others say sickness is just a part of the world we live in. So who is right?

Let us examine a few of the passages which have been used by all sides to support their beliefs.

> Numbers 14:12
> *I will strike them down with a plague and destroy them, but I will make you into a nation greater and stronger than they.*

> Exodus 4:11
> *The Lord said to him, Who gave human beings their mouths? Who makes them deaf or mute? Who gives them sight or makes them blind? Is it not I, the Lord?*

Taking those passages at face value, they would be saying God sends plagues and makes people deaf and mute. Other passages including plagues can be found in Exodus, chapters 7–11. Who sent those plagues? God did.

On the other side, we have many stories of Satan being the author of the sickness.

See the story of a woman crippled by a demon in *Luke 13:10–11, "On a Sabbath Jesus was teaching in one of the synagogues, and a woman was there who had been crippled by a spirit for eighteen years. She was bent over and could not straighten up at all."* Who crippled this woman? A demon.

A seizure caused by a demon. *Luke 9:39–40, "A spirit seizes him and he suddenly screams; it throws him into convulsions so that he foams at the mouth. It scarcely ever leaves him and is destroying him. I begged your disciples to drive it out, but they could not"* Who gave the man a seizure? A demon.

A man made insane by a demon. *Luke 8:27, "When Jesus stepped ashore, he was met by a demon-possessed man from the town. For a long time this man had not worn clothes or lived in a house, but had lived in the tombs."* Who made the man insane? A demon.

A man who could not speak because of a demon. *Luke 11:14, "Jesus was driving out a demon that was mute. When the demon left, the man who had been mute spoke, and the crowd was amazed."*

A note of interest: The man was not dumb. The demon inside the man was dumb. Once the dumb demon was driven out, the man spoke.

Finally, there is the story of a man cutting himself by a demon in *Mark 5:5, "Night and day among the tombs and in the hills* he would cry out and cut himself with stones."

Having a spirit of discernment is paramount here because we know not every situation is the result of God punishing someone or is demon-caused.

My point to all of this is that when it comes to understanding tragedy and health challenges, there are many variables to consider.

(For more information see also Luke 13:11, Luke 13:16, Matthew 10:1, Acts 10:37–38, and 2 Corinthians 12:7.)

I know some people will disagree with some of my conclusion, but based on Scripture, that is my take.

What I would like to convey to the world about this disagreement among believers is our ability to disagree and still love each other. We call this an *in-house* disagreement. It is also important to know that when it comes to the essentials of the gospel, we are all in agreement. The issues we disagree on have no bearing on one's salvation.

The truth is that no matter what the situation, for the true believer, what the devil meant for evil, God can turn around for His glory.

Key #13 Who Is the Author of Sickness?

- KEY #14 -

THE JOB FACTOR

The book of Job is a very difficult book to tackle. I want to briefly give my perspective on this book because over the years I have heard many different sermons addressing the subject of Job and suffering. Our belief on this difficult book can cause us to deceive ourselves when it comes to dealing with various health challenges. Reading through the Bible, I have encountered many passages that I have difficulty understanding. Job is one such book. At the same time, I accept these books by faith, and have no problem admitting that I have difficulty with them.

Many of my friends use the book of Job to build a case regarding suffering. They believe that the suffering Job encountered happened as a result of what he said in verse 25 of chapter 3. I could not disagree more. Let us examine this verse, *"What I feared has come upon me; what I dreaded has happened to me."*

My friends believe that Job's negative confession was what caused the family tragedy he experienced to happen. I love my friends, but I totally disagree with their conclusion.

Let us take a closer look at this passage, because it is important. In Job 1:6–7, we find the angels and the devil appearing before God, *"One day the angels came to present themselves before the Lord and Satan also came with them."*

This means that the devil still has access to the throne of God. I cannot explain this verse. I just have to accept it for what it says.

Another Scripture that supports this is found in Revelations 12:10, *"And I heard a loud voice saying in heaven, Now is come salvation, and strength, and the kingdom of our God, and the power of his Christ: for the accuser of our brethren is cast down, which accused them before our God day and night."*

The Lord asked Satan what he thought of Job, a man He called blameless and upright. Satan answered in *Job 1:10, "Have you not put a hedge around him and his household and everything he has? You have blessed the work of his hands, so that his flocks and herds are spread throughout the land,"* Satan was saying to God, "Job is praising you because you have blessed and protected him by placing a hedge of protection around him. Take away your protection and see what happens." *"The Lord said to Satan, 'Very well, then, everything he has is in your power, but on the man himself do not lay a finger'"* (Job 1:12).

Did Job's negative confession in Job 3:25 allow the devil to appear before God with the angels?

Did Job's negative confession cause God to ask the devil about him? Did Job's negative confession cause God to remove His protection? The answer to all these questions is no.

God was not talking to the devil about Job's "negative" confession. If God should remove his protection from any of us, we would all be in serious trouble. If all the devil needs to wreak havoc in our lives is a negative confession, he would have killed many believers already. I know many people who love Jesus and have had negative confessions. If that was all the devil needed, they would all be gone by now.

The Scripture continues the narrative and tells us the devil then left God's presence, knowing Job's protection was gone and inflicted major damage on Job and his family.

In Job 2:3, the devil makes a return trip to see God. *"Then the LORD said to Satan, "Have you considered my servant Job? There is no one on earth like him; he is blameless and upright, a man who fears God and shuns evil. And he still maintains his integrity, though you incited me against him to ruin him without any reason."*

Pay close attention to the last part that says *you incited me against him without any reason.* God did not say Job's confession had anything to do with his situation. When God said there was no reason and that he was blameless and upright, how can we now say the opposite?

In the end, God reprimanded Job's friends for their words.

> Job 42:7
> *After the Lord had said these things to Job, he said to Eliphaz the Temanite, I am angry with you and your two friends, because you have not spoken the truth about me, as my servant Job has.*

If my children did something wrong that caused unprecedented suffering, I would tell them what they did so they would not repeat the same mistake again. Notice God never said to Job, "What happened to you was a result of your mouth and your negative confession." We need to do the same. This story is not the norm we see in Scripture. We just have to trust God on this one.

Key #14 The Job Factor

- KEY #15 -

CHOOSE YOUR ADVISORS CAREFULLY

Who are your advisors?

When difficult decisions have to be made, to whom do you look to for counsel?

Wisdom means we do not deceive ourselves into believing we are always right or have all the answers. No one person will have all the answers. That is why it is important to choose our advisors carefully.

With that in mind, ask yourself one question: "Who are my advisors?

Keep in mind that just because someone is a "Christian" does not mean he or she will give you good advice. Here are a few examples:

1 Kings 13, Young Prophet (a believer) listened to an old Prophet (another believer) and that advice cost the young Prophet his life.

Genesis 41, Pharaoh (a nonbeliever) listened to Joseph (a believer) and saved an entire nation.

2 Chronicles 35:20–36, Josiah (a believer) did not listen to Neco (a nonbeliever), and this cost him his life.

Esther 5:14, Haman listened to his wife and friends and was executed on the gallows that **they told him to build**. The counsel of his wife and friends cost him his life.

Acts 27:11, The centurion (a nonbeliever) did not listen to Paul (a believer) and lost the cargo and the ship.

Non-Christians can have wisdom, faith, and a spirit of discernment too. The question we all have to answer is, apart from hearing the voice of God for ourselves, to whom do we listen?

King Saul was being tormented by demons. Interestingly, the servants were the ones who were able to correctly diagnose his problem and recommend a solution. What is even more remarkable is that Saul did not say, "You are servants; I am not listening to you." He took their advice—which worked.

> 1 Samuel 16:15–16
> *And Saul's servants said unto him, Behold now, an evil spirit from God troubleth thee. Let our lord now command thy servants, which are before thee, to seek out a man, who is a cunning player on a harp: and it shall come to pass, when the evil spirit from God is upon thee, that he shall play with his hand, and thou shalt be well.*

One of the secrets for avoiding deception is learning how to discern through whom God is speaking. God could speak through a leader, or He might speak through a servant. Our responsibility is to discern through whom He is speaking.

Naaman, a nonbeliever, was healed from leprosy. Why? Because he listened to his wife, who listened to a servant girl (2 Kings 5).

We have to make sure we are listening to the right people, because listening to the wrong person can have catastrophic consequences.

King Ahaziah gave us a clear example in *2 Chronicles 22:3–4:*

> *He too walked in the ways of the house of Ahab, for his mother encouraged him in doing wrong. He did evil in the eyes of the Lord, as the house of Ahab had done, for after his father's death they became his advisors to his undoing."*

Key #15 Choose Your Advisors Carefully

NOT BECAUSE THEY ARE MANY, MEANS THEY ARE RIGHT

One of the most tragic stories of deception is found in Numbers 16. Korah got upset with Moses and brought 250 well-known community leaders to challenge him. He told Moses the entire community was holy and that God was with them. **They were leaders, they were famous, and there were many.**

Looking from the outside, one could say, "These are our leaders, and they are all in agreement against the man of God. This means they are right and Moses is wrong."

The same is happening today. Many people are following the wrong leaders and don't know it. That is deception. Leaders are giving *their versions* of truth, and they have many famous, well-known people supporting their theories. We all need to know that truth is not necessarily found in fame, numbers, or status.

There are many deceived people walking around saying they are Christians, but are they really?

Korah should have thought this through thoroughly, but he didn't. He thought the entire community was holy, but he was deceived.

Moses was not deceived. He told Korah and his followers to appear before God the next day. Moses was going to allow

God to prove who was holy. Korah's deception was so great that he and all his followers showed up to challenge Moses.

God showed up, and I imagine in Korah's mind he was saying, "I am going to fix Moses, because God will show him that I was right, and he was wrong." Korah had no idea he was deceived and how dangerous this can be. As I wrote earlier, **"Deception is believing you are right, but you are wrong and you don't know it."**

Korah's deception was in the process of being uncovered.

Numbers 16:23–24
Then the Lord *said to Moses, 'Say to the assembly, 'Move away from the tents of Korah, Dathan and Abiram.'*

As soon as those words were uttered, everyone knew there was a major problem. The chapter continues

Numbers 16:28–35 NIV
Then Moses said, "This is how you will know that the Lord has sent me to do all these things and that it was not my idea: If these men die a natural death and experience only what usually happens to men, then the Lord has not sent me. But if the Lord brings about something totally new, and the earth opens its mouth and swallows them, with everything that belongs to them, and they go down alive into the grave, then you will know that these men have treated the Lord with contempt."

As soon as he finished saying all this, the ground under them split apart and the earth opened its mouth and swallowed them, with their households and all Korah's men and all their

possessions. They went down alive into the grave, with everything they owned; the earth closed over them, and they perished and were gone from the community. At their cries, all the Israelites around them fled, shouting, "The earth is going to swallow us too!" And fire came out from the Lord and consumed the 250 men who were offering the incense.

The root of deception can be very deep, and once you get there, it's difficult to untangle yourself.

One would think everyone would get the message that not everyone saying they are God's people are actually God's people—but not Korah's friends. Let's take a look at what happened the following day.

Numbers 16:41–42
The next day the whole Israelite community grumbled against Moses and Aaron. 'You have killed the Lord's people,' they said. But when the assembly gathered in opposition to Moses and Aaron and turned toward the Tent of Meeting, suddenly the cloud covered it and the glory of the Lord appeared."

This is amazing to me. The people watched the confrontation between Korah and Moses. God appeared and showed who was deceived. The people witnessed all this, yet still they showed up the next day accusing Moses of killing the Lord's people.

What would cause this? Deception.

The truth was, Korah and his followers were dead because Korah and his followers were deceived. Korah told Moses that the people were holy and that the Lord was with them. The fact is, they were not holy, and the Lord was not with them.

God then showed up again *Numbers 16:43–50:*

> *Then Moses and Aaron went to the front of the tent of meeting, and the Lord said to Moses, Get away from this assembly so I can put an end to them at once. And they fell facedown. Then Moses said to Aaron, Take your censer and put incense in it, along with burning coals from the altar, and hurry to the assembly to make atonement for them. Wrath has come out from the Lord; the plague has started. So Aaron did as Moses said, and ran into the midst of the assembly. The plague had already started among the people, but Aaron offered the incense and made atonement for them. He stood between the living and the dead, and the plague stopped. But 14,700 people died from the plague, in addition to those who had died because of Korah. Then Aaron returned to Moses at the entrance to the tent of meeting, for the plague had stopped.*

Korah's deception cost the lives of almost 15,000 people.

Key #16 Not Because They Are Many, Means They Are Right

- KEY #17 -

THE DANGER OF FALSE WORSHIP

When one encounters the word *danger,* it's time to stop, think, ponder, and examine. It's time to make sure we know and understand what we are being warned about.

I purposely entitled this key, "The Danger of False Worship" because I believe it is dangerous to overlook false worship by invoking grace. Like I wrote earlier, many deceived people have said we are under grace, so we can basically live any way we want. That is deceptive and dangerous thinking.

When it comes to worship, we need to ask a few questions.

* What is worship?

* Does God approve of our worship?

* If He does, how do we know?

You can sing songs *about* God, or you can sing songs *to* God. **Are you offering to God the worship that He sanctions?**

There is false worship, and there is true worship. In order to know what's false, we need to know what is true.

At home we don't have to tell our kids that a glass is dirty. All we have to do is put a clean glass beside the dirty one, and they will see the difference. You cannot have a false product unless you have a real product. There is true worship, and there is false worship. True worship originates with God. He is the one who created worship and told us that this pleased Him.

So the question is, "What is true worship?"

True worship is applauding God for who He is. Worship is an expression of love and devotion to God.

The word *worship* is used hundreds of times in the Bible. Worship is such an important word that God said He is looking for a certain kind of worshiper.

> John 4:23–24
> *Yet a time is coming and has now come when the true worshipers will worship the Father in spirit and truth, for they are the kind of worshipers the Father seeks. God is spirit, and his worshipers must worship in spirit and in truth.*

Jesus is saying true worshippers worship God in spirit and in truth. The problem with deception and false worship is that we can convince ourselves we are worshipping God, but the truth is we are not worshipping God, and our worship is going nowhere. God is not accepting our worship, and we don't know it. That is deception.

Once I was ministering at a church and encountered a unique situation. The pastor had changed the worship format and as a result many people became angry. They never left the church, but their anger led them to boycott the worship service.

Each Sunday they would come to church and stay in the lobby until the worship time was over before they would join the rest of the service.

I witnessed this, and I felt the Lord speak to my spirit. He shared with me that the people boycotting the worship time did not understand worship. He then gave me an example using food.

For each person reading this book, take this journey with me. I believe that this journey will help us to clearly understand what God wants us to know about true worship.

Ask yourself this question: "What food do I not like?" Select a food and make sure it is something that you really dislike. Now that you have identified this food, think about what you would do if I visited you and brought a present of the food you do not like; what would you say to me? I am sure you would be kind and tell me, "Thanks, but no thanks."

What if on my next visit the next week, I brought for you the same food that you do not like? What would you do? What would happen if week after week, month after month, year after year I kept bringing for you the same food you do not like?

I am sure sooner or later you would become angry with me and tell me that I have no respect for you. Why? Because I am trying to force you to accept what you do not like.

The Lord then explained that it is the same with worship. Worship is not about what *we* like. **Worship is about God and what He likes.** God is the one who designed and created worship. I cannot tell Him what to like. He is God. If we are truly going to worship in spirit and in truth, we have to find out what God likes and then offer that to Him.

Many people deceive themselves by believing that if they shout, raise their hands, or say "Amen," then that's worship.

Others are part of a choir singing gospel music, and they believe because they dance, shout, and say "Hallelujah," they are worshipping God.

I do not want you to misunderstand what I am saying. I believe in exuberant praise. I believe in raising hands, saying "Amen," shouting "Hallelujah," and dancing. At the same time that does not mean that you are worshiping God. Just like being in a quiet reflective service singing "Holy, Holy" does not mean you are worshipping, either.

There are many people deceiving themselves and faking the anointing. They have no clue what it means to have a personal relationship with Jesus, but they are singing about Jesus. They are faking the anointing.

Faking the anointing means the person is preaching or singing and acting like the Holy Spirit is present. Many have deceived themselves into believing that the Holy Spirit is present, but what is really present is an emotional demonstration based on the flesh.

One major gospel artist confessed that he was singing gospel music a long time before he got saved. Many people thought he was saved and anointed. At the same time, he himself knew he was faking it, but he did not tell anyone until later.

Let us examine our own hearts and make sure God is pleased with our worship. Start with God and then examine your heart.

Matthew 15:8–9
These people honor me with their lips, but their hearts are far from me. They worship me in vain; their teachings are merely human rules.

Amos 5:21–23
I hate, I despise your religious festivals; your assemblies are a stench to me. Even though you

bring me burnt offerings and grain offerings, I will not accept them. Though you bring choice fellowship offerings, I will have no regard for them. Away with the noise of your songs! I will not listen to the music of your harps.

God was telling the people that their worship was not pleasing to Him. I imagine God is saying the same thing today to many people.

It is also important to know that sincerity (even though important) is not what God is looking for in worship. God is looking for obedience. David discovered this the hard way.

2 Samuel 6:3–7
They set the ark of God on a new cart and brought it from the house of Abinadab, which was on the hill. Uzzah and Ahio, sons of Abinadab, were guiding the new cart with the ark of God on it, and Ahio was walking in front of it. David and the whole house of Israel were celebrating with all their might before the Lord, with songs and with harps, lyres, tambourines, sistrums and cymbals.

When they came to the threshing floor of Nacon, Uzzah reached out and took hold of the ark of God, because the oxen stumbled. The Lord's anger burned against Uzzah because of his irreverent act; therefore God struck him down and he died there beside the ark of God.

The worship looked great. David and the people were dancing, the musicians were playing, and singers were singing and praising God. There was a major problem, and no one knew it until Uzzah was killed.

Here David explains the problem, and why Uzzah was killed.

1 Chronicles 15:13–15
It was because you, the Levites, did not bring it up the first time that the LORD our God broke out in anger against us. We did not inquire of him about how to do it in the prescribed way. So the priests and Levites consecrated themselves in order to bring up the ark of the LORD, the God of Israel. And the Levites carried the ark of God with the poles on their shoulders, as Moses had commanded in accordance with the word of the LORD.

Notice the choice of words David used. He said we did not inquire of the Lord about how to do it in the prescribed way. David's idea was to put the ark of God on a brand new cart. God was saying, "That is what you like. That is not what I like. What I like is for the Levites to carry the ark with poles on their shoulders." Not understanding this key cost Uzzah his life.

Let us give God true worship—worship that He sanctions. We must always worship in spirit and truth. Let us make sure we do not deceive ourselves with false worship, hoping God will accept it. He will not.

Key #17 The Danger of False Worship

- KEY #18 -

WALK BY THE SPIRIT

What does it really mean to walk by the Spirit?

It means living by the unction and leading of the precious Holy Spirit. It means leaving your comfort zone and many times operating on a level that defies human logic. It means walking by tapping into a supernatural Person who will guide you and keep you from being deceived.

People who are deceived in the natural realm are deceived by what they see and hear. Your natural senses can deceive you.

God sent Samuel to anoint a new king. As soon as he got there, he encountered a war between his natural sense and his spiritual senses.

> 1 Samuel 16:3, 6–7
> *Invite Jesse to the sacrifice, and I will show you what to do. You are to anoint for me the one I indicate. When they arrived, Samuel saw Eliab and thought, 'Surely the Lord's anointed stands here before the Lord.' But the Lord said to Samuel, 'Do not consider his appearance or his height, for I have rejected him.' The Lord does not look at the things people look at. People look at the outward appearance, but the Lord looks at the heart.*

Samuel, looking with his natural eyes, thought Eliab was the right person, but God spoke to his spirit and said, "Eliab is not the one." Samuel knew the voice of God, so when God spoke to his spirit, he obeyed. We must remember that God's ways are not our ways.

God could have said to Samuel, "Go and anoint Jesse's son David," but He didn't. He allowed Samuel to make the trip, having no idea who God was going to pick. Even after rejecting Eliab, God could have said, "Look for David," but He did not. He allowed the selection process to go forward. Why?

We are not told why God did this, but I believe the journey is just as important to God as the destination. Our responsibility is not to know the *why*. Our duty is to walk in obedience to the word the Lord gave us.

A few years ago, I was privileged to minister at a maximum security prison. While there, I visited death row. During this visit I spoke to two inmates. They both talked about the Lord and knew Scripture. The problem was, my spirit could relate to one of the men, but I had difficulty relating to the other. Something was wrong, but I could not put my finger on it. Both were saying the right things and quoting Scripture, but my spirit was troubled by one.

After leaving death row, the chaplain asked me if I knew the gentleman I was talking to, and I told him I did not.

He said the man was a serial killer, and gave me his name to look up. I did, and could not believe what I uncovered. This guy was a notorious serial killer in America. The chaplain believed that he has murdered over twenty people. Even though he talked Scripture, I now understood why my spirit had difficulty relating to him. I knew something was not right.

Please do not misunderstand what I am saying. I know God

can forgive anyone—even the worst serial killer. The difference for me was I got a check in my spirit. When that happens, I have learned not to overlook it. Listening and watching with my natural ears and eyes would have caused me to say this was a brother in Christ. But with a major check in my spirit, I decided to leave that call up to God.

Paul encountered a similar situation in Acts 16:16–18, *"Once when we were going to the place of prayer we were met by a slave girl who had a spirit by which she predicted the future. She earned a great deal of money for her owners by fortune-telling. She followed Paul and the rest of us, shouting, 'These men are servants of the Most High God, who are telling you the way to be saved.' She kept this up for many days. Finally Paul became so troubled that he turned around and said to the spirit, 'In the name of Jesus Christ I command you to come out of her!' At that moment the spirit left her."*

Paul did a very good thing by casting the unclean spirit out, so what was the problem? What the girl said was true. She said, "These men are servants of the Most High God, who are telling you the way to be saved."

That's the truth, so what was the problem? The problem was her words were true, but the source was wrong.

Paul, walking with a spirit of discernment, was able to detect that this girl had an unholy spirit. Verse 18 says, *"Finally Paul became so troubled that he turned around and said to the spirit, 'Come out of her.'"*

Important note: Paul did not deal with the girl; he dealt with the spirit. We need to do the same. That's why Ephesians 6:12 says, *"For we wrestle not against flesh and blood, but against principalities, against powers, against the rulers of the darkness of this world, against spiritual wickedness in high places."*

Paul was not fighting against the girl. He was fighting against the demonic spirit that was influencing her. We need to follow Paul's example.

If there ever was a time for us to walk by the Spirit, it is now. There are many voices speaking, and walking by the Spirit allows us to hear clearly through whom God is really speaking.

Many people have made major mistakes because they allowed their natural senses to deceive them.

Have you ever met someone and he or she seems like a nice person, but in your spirit you keep saying, "This is a great person, but there is just something that I cannot put my finger on?" When that happens, you have to walk by the Spirit.

This is critical in the business world. You might be hiring, and the person looks the part and says all the right things. The only problem is, you keep getting a check in your spirit. When that happens, here is what I would recommend:

• Take time out to pray for God's direction.

• Consult your most trusted advisers. Make sure you have a few people in your life that you trust. Ask them to join you in praying about the situation.

• Take your time to make this decision. Hasty decisions can have costly consequences.

• Do not go with your natural eyes; trust your spirit and ask the Holy Spirit to guide you.

Walking by the Spirit will guard us against deception.

Key #18 Walk By The Spirit

INQUIRE OF THE LORD

"I thought this was what you wanted."

"What gave you that idea?"

"I don't know. I just thought so." "Why didn't you ask me?"

"I don't know. I will do that next time."

Have you had that conversation before? Many have been deceived and made bad decisions because they failed to inquire of the person and of the Lord.

In Joshua 9, we find the story of the Gibeonites' deception. The children of Israel were conquering lands everywhere they went. The size of the opposing armies was no factor in their victories or defeats.

Their victories were all tied to these two things: inquiring of God and then walking in total obedience.

As a result of their failure to do this, they were deceived. *Joshua 9:3–6, "However, when the people of Gibeon heard what Joshua had done to Jericho and Ai, they resorted to a ruse: They went as a delegation whose donkeys were loaded with worn-out sacks and old wineskins, cracked and mended.*

They put worn and patched sandals on their feet and wore old clothes. All the bread of their food supply was dry and moldy. Then they went to Joshua in the camp at Gilgal and said to him and the Israelites, 'We have come from a distant country; make a treaty with us.'"

The Gibeonite deception was based on false pretenses, fake emotions, lies, and Israel's inability to use the *spirit test* instead of the *eye test.*

The Gibeonites knew the army of Israel would be moved by their plight. So they put on worn-out clothes and worn-out shoes, carried moldy bread, and had a well-thought-out story to complete their deception. To their amazement, it worked. They were able to deceive Israel.

The answer for the army of Israel being deceived is found in Joshua 9:14, *"The Israelites sampled their provisions but did not inquire of the Lord."*

One of the keys in guarding against deception is to make sure we inquire of the Lord.

Do you inquire of the Lord when you make your decisions?

Many times at home, I have been reminded by my children of this key. I must admit, there has been a time in the past when I lost something and was feverishly searching for it. I solicited the help of my children, and very soon one would say, "Dad, did you pray about it? Did you inquire of the Lord?"

In my flesh I would think, *Come on, just help me search,* but I have learned over the years that prayer works even for seemingly trivial stuff. Finally I will stop and pray, and shortly thereafter the item would be found.

There are many verses that cover this very important key.

2 Samuel 2:1 says, "In the course of time, David inquired of the Lord. Shall I go up to one of the towns of Judah?' he asked. The Lord said, 'Go up.' David asked, 'Where shall I go?' 'To Hebron,' the Lord answered."

David wanted to know a location, so he inquired of God.

Many times, people move without consulting God and very soon realize they have made a huge mistake. Let us learn from the example of David. *2 Samuel 5:18–19, "Now the Philistines had come and spread out in the Valley of Rephaim; so David inquired of the Lord, 'Shall I go and attack the Philistines? Will you deliver them into my hands?' The Lord answered him, 'Go, for I will surely deliver the Philistines into your hands.'"*

David wanted to know if he should go to war or not. God gave him clear instructions.

> 2 Samuel 5:22–23
> *Once more the Philistines came up and spread out in the Valley of Rephaim; so David inquired of the Lord, and he answered, Do not go straight up, but circle around behind them and attack them in front of the poplar trees.*

This is a very important verse because when David inquired of the Lord, he got different instructions this time. The first time, God said, "Yes, go and fight."

This time God said, "Don't go straight up, but circle from behind." **Victory in every area of our lives rests with us inquiring, hearing, and obeying the voice of God.**

> 1 Samuel 30:8
> *And David inquired of the Lord, 'Shall I pursue this raiding party? Will I overtake them? Pursue*

them,' he answered. You will certainly overtake them and succeed in the rescue.

2 Chronicles 20:2–3
Some people came and told Jehoshaphat, 'A vast army is coming against you from Edom, from the other side of the Dead Sea. It is already in Hazezon Tamar' (that is, En Gedi). Alarmed, Jehoshaphat resolved to inquire of the Lord, and he proclaimed a fast for all Judah.

2 Chronicles 18:3–4
Ahab king of Israel asked Jehoshaphat king of Judah, Will you go with me against Ramoth Gilead? Jehoshaphat replied, I am as you are, and my people as your people; we will join you in the war. But Jehoshaphat also said to the king of Israel, 'First seek the counsel of the Lord.

2 Samuel 21:1
There was a three-year famine in the days of David, year after year; and David inquired of the Lord. The Lord replied, It is on account of Saul and his bloody house, for he put to death the Gibeonites.

This is a very interesting passage. There was a natural disaster affecting the land. Instead of just saying, "This is a natural disaster," David sought the Lord for a spiritual answer. God told him this disaster was a result of what Saul had done to the Gibeonites.

In another book I will cover the subject of natural disasters. For the sake of this book, I would like to make a quick point: Natural disasters happen all the time. Every year there are earthquakes, storms, famines, hurricanes, and fires. How do we know when a "natural" disaster has spiritual significance or if it is just a natural occurrence? What is the litmus test one uses to determine if it is natural or spiritual? The main point I want to make is that when there are natural disasters, there can be spiritual significance.

I am not saying all natural disasters have spiritual significance. However, we must recognize from Scripture that this could be the case. With this in mind, we need to walk with a spirit of discernment and inquire of the Lord when it comes to this issue.

Another story supporting this theory that disasters can have spiritual significance is found in the book of Jonah. Jonah and the sailors were caught in the midst of a storm, the magnitude of which they had never seen. *Jonah 1:7–8, "Then the sailors said to each other, 'Come, let us cast lots to find out who is responsible for this calamity.' They cast lots and the lot fell on Jonah. So they asked him, 'Tell us, who is responsible for making all this trouble for us? What kind of work do you do? Where do you come from? What is your country? From what people are you?'"*

Wow! These are amazing questions in the face of a natural disaster. The fisherman knew the natural storm was not natural. That's why they asked the questions that they did. What kind of questions are these in the midst of a natural crisis?

Let us cast lots to find who is responsible? This response is very interesting. The amazing thing is that their hunch was right. Jonah's disobedience was the cause of that natural disaster.

If we inquire of God by consulting Him in all our decisions, that will keep us from being deceived. In 1 Kings 14 we see a failed attempt at deception.

At that time Abijah son of Jeroboam became ill, and Jeroboam said to his wife, Go, disguise yourself, so you won't be recognized as the wife of Jeroboam. Then go to Shiloh. Ahijah the prophet is there—the one who told me I would be king over this people. Take ten loaves of bread with you, some cakes and a jar of honey, and go to him. He will tell you what will happen to the boy. So Jeroboam's wife did what he said and went to Ahijah's house in Shiloh. Now Ahijah could not see; his sight was gone because of his age. But the Lord had told Ahijah, Jeroboam's wife is coming to ask you about her son, for he is ill, and you are to give her such and such an answer. When she arrives, she will pretend to be someone else.

I have a few important observations. This deception was being carried out against a blind person. Even so, it failed because in God's kingdom we are not led by our natural eyes. God's kingdom is a Spirit-led kingdom, and the more we train ourselves to be Spirit-led and not sight-led, the more we will guard against deception.

This showcases the need to hear the voice of God for ourselves. That's what the prophet Ahijah did, and it kept him from being deceived. The Lord told Ahijah exactly what was about to happen, so he was able to avoid the deception.

The Lord will tell us, too. We just have to train ourselves to hear His voice for ourselves, and the starting point is making sure we inquire of the Lord.

Key #19 Inquire of the Lord

- *KEY #20* -

HINDRANCES TO PRAYER

Prayer is the most powerful weapon in the believer's arsenal. Having a consistent and powerful prayer life is critical for success in our daily lives. There are many books written on prayer, but it's important to note that prayer is not an exact science. There are many variables to consider when it comes to prayer.

When you pray and don't get the answer you wanted, what do you do? What goes through your mind? Understanding the importance of this key is crucial because there are many factors to be considered when it comes to prayer.

It's also important to know that saying we are Christians does not guarantee victory. What guarantees victory is our obedience to the instructions God gives us.

There are many people fasting, praying, and believing God for a miracle. Many deceive themselves into believing that the reason their prayers are not answered is because God is saying, "My grace is sufficient for you. Just hang on for my perfect timing, and you will see the results."

Don't get me wrong—this could be true. This is addressed in 2 Corinthians 12:8–9, *"Three times I pleaded with the Lord to take it away from me. But He said to me, My grace is sufficient for you, for my power is made perfect in weakness.' Thereforen*

I will boast all the more gladly about my weaknesses, so that Christ's power may rest on me."

On the other side, the problem could be that the person is living with unconfessed sin or walking in total rebellion. It is important to know that there is:

• A time to pray

• A time to wait

• A time to fast

• A time not to pray

I am sure you are saying, *"Did he really say a time* not to *pray?"* Yes, you read that right. There is a time not to pray. How can that be when we are commanded to pray without ceasing? *1 Thessalonians 5:17, "Pray without ceasing."* Yes, that's true, but there is also a time not to pray. This is addressed in Joshua 6–7.

God gave the children of Israel clear instructions for a battle they were about to fight. *Joshua 6:18, "But keep away from the devoted things, so that you will not bring about your own destruction by taking any of them. Otherwise you will make the camp of Israel liable to destruction and bring trouble on it. All the silver and gold and the articles of bronze and iron are sacred to the Lord and must go into his treasury."*

God told them to keep away from the devoted things, but Achan disobeyed. *Joshua 7:1, "But the Israelites were unfaithful in regard to the devoted things; Achan son of Karmi, the son of Zimri, the son of Zerah, of the tribe of Judah, took some of them. So the Lord's anger burned against Israel."*

Without knowing there was sin in the camp, Joshua sent the

army into the next battle against an inferior army. They lost the battle. As a result of this loss, Joshua and the elders of Israel tore their clothes, sprinkled dust on their heads (which was a sign of distress), and prayed until evening. *Joshua 7:6, "Then Joshua tore his clothes and fell facedown to the ground before the ark of the* Lord, *remaining there till evening. The elders of Israel did the same, and sprinkled dust on their heads."*

Finally God showed up and made a very interesting statement. *Joshua 7:10, "The* Lord *said to Joshua, Stand up! What are you doing down on your face?'"* What kind of a question is this?

Of course, God knew Joshua and the leaders were praying, but God was saying, "Stop praying. Now is not the time to pray."

God then explains to them why they lost and also what they should do. *Joshua 7:12–13, "That is why the Israelites cannot stand against their enemies; they turn their backs and run because they have been made liable to destruction. I will not be with you anymore unless you destroy whatever among you is devoted to destruction. Go, consecrate the people. Tell them, 'Consecrate yourselves in preparation for tomorrow; for this is what the* Lord, *the God of Israel, says: There are devoted things among you, Israel. You cannot stand against your enemies until you remove them.'"*

In essence, God was saying, "You can fast, pray, and sprinkle dust on your head, but until you stop praying and take action by obeying Me, you will not be able to stand against your enemies."

Every believer will sin, but if we continue to live in sin, we cannot expect our prayers to be answered.

Many people deceive themselves into believing they can live any way they want to live and expect God to answer their prayers because they are under grace. **Living under grace does not give us a blank check or unfettered license to sin.**

> Romans 6:1–2 (NIV)
> *What shall we say, then? Shall we go on sinning so that grace may increase? By no means! We are those who have died to sin; how can we live in it any longer?*

> Ephesians 5:6
> *Let no one deceive you with empty words, for because of such things God's wrath comes on those who are disobedient.*

I am amazed that there are not more sermons calling for holiness. A lot of what I am hearing is simply focused on grace. Like I mentioned, we are all grateful for grace. We all need it in our lives. At the same time we can't deceive ourselves into accepting the belief that there are no consequences for sin.

If there was no consequence for sins now, why would God kill Ananias and Sapphira in Acts 5:1–11? Keep in mind that this happened after Jesus had paid the price for their sins.

1 Corinthians 11:27–30 warns us about taking the communion in an unworthy manner, *"For anyone who eats and drinks without recognizing the body of the Lord eats and drinks judgment on himself. That is why many among you are weak and sick and some have fallen asleep."* Another way of saying that they died is that they have "fallen asleep."

Anyone who believes that because of grace they can live any way they want is living under deception. Living this way will only affect your life and hinder your prayers.

There are many things that can inhibit our prayers.

Here are a few more:

Psalm 66:18
If I regard iniquity in my heart, the Lord will not hear me.

Do you regard iniquity in your heart? This will hinder your prayers.

1 Peter 3:7
Husbands, in the same way be considerate as you live with your wives, and treat them with respect as the weaker partner and as heirs with you of the gracious gift of life, so that nothing will hinder your prayers.

Do you treat your spouse improperly? This will hinder your prayers.

Isaiah 59:2
But your iniquities have separated you from your God; your sins have hidden his face from you, so that he will not hear.

Are your iniquities or sins hindering your prayers?

Zechariah 7:13
When I called, they did not listen; so when they called, I would not listen,' says the Lord Almighty.

Are you walking in disobedience by not listening to God? That will hinder your prayers.

Proverbs 28:9
If anyone turns a deaf ear to my instruction, even their prayers are detestable."

Are you turning your ears away from God's commands? That will hinder your prayers.

> Proverbs 1:28–30
> *Then they will call to me but I will not answer; they will look for me but will not find me, since they hated knowledge and did not choose to fear the Lord. Since they would not accept my advice and spurned my rebuke.*

Do you hate knowledge and do not fear the Lord? This will hinder your prayers.

> Isaiah 58:3–4 (NIV)
> *Why have we fasted, they say, and you have not seen it? Why have we humbled ourselves, and you have not noticed?' Yet on the day of your fasting, you do as you please and exploit all your workers. Your fasting ends in quarreling and strife, and in striking each other with wicked fists. You cannot fast as you do today and expect your voice to be heard on high.*

Do you exploit those who work for you? Are you fasting in accordance with Biblical mandate? This will hinder your prayers.

Let us not casually dismiss these verses and say that they are not applicable today. They *are*. Let us make sure that we are Spiritually in line with God's Word, and that there is nothing hindering our prayers.

Key #20 Hindrances to Prayer

Keys For Living
PART THREE

- KEY #21 -

KNOW YOUR INSTRUMENT: KNOW THE WORD

There is a dangerous condition in flying called *vertigo*. This happens when a pilot in midflight gets disoriented. When this happens, the pilot cannot tell the difference between up and down. At this point there is only one way to survive.

The pilot has to make a decision beforehand that no matter what he or she sees, no matter what is heard or felt, no matter what the conditions are, no matter the advice of friends or fellow passengers, that pilot is going to do one thing: **trust the instruments.**

The pilot is going to take a look at the instruments and do whatever the instruments direct. Failure to do this can have catastrophic consequences.

As Christians, our instrument is the Word of God. It does not matter what our leaders say or do. It does not matter what our friends or family members say or do. It does not matter if it's popular or has been approved by the world. When the world and the Word clash, go with the Word. Ask one question: **What does the Word say?**

The Word is the solid foundation upon which we can build our lives to guard against deception. The Scripture says in Matthew 24:35, *"Heaven and earth will pass away, but my words will never pass away."*

2 Timothy 2:15
Study to shew thyself approved unto God, a
workman that needeth not to be ashamed,
rightly dividing the word of truth.

To guard against deception, we need to know what the Word
says. If you do not know what the Word says, how can you
draw a credible conclusion based on speculation?

The Word lists a group of deceived people we need to be aware
of. Before listing the group, we need to remember that it is not
our job to label people. That is the work of the Lord. Our job
is to know the Word and then allow the precious Holy Spirit
to give us the accurate interpretation. *John 16:13, "But when
he, the Spirit of truth, comes, he will guide you into all the
truth. He will not speak on his own; he will speak only what
he hears, and he will tell you what is yet to come."*

Here is a partial list:

Titus 1:16
*They claim to know God, but by their actions
they deny him. They are detestable, disobedient
and unfit for doing anything good.*

Who are these people who claim to know God but deny Him
by their actions?

Matthew 7:15–16
*Watch out for false prophets. They come to you
in sheep's clothing, but inwardly they are
ferocious wolves. By their fruit you will recognize
them. Do people pick grapes from thornbushes,
or figs from thistles?*

Who are these false prophets that come to us in sheep
clothing? Using sheep clothing is an attempt at deception. It is

a disguise to cover the person's true identity. Be on your guard.

1 John 4:1
Dear friends, do not believe every spirit, but test the spirits to see whether they are from God, because many false prophets have gone out into the world.

2 Timothy 4:3–4
For the time will come when people will not put up with sound doctrine. Instead, to suit their own desires, they will gather around them a great number of teachers to say what their itching ears want to hear. They will turn their ears away from the truth and turn aside to myths.

The problem here is twofold. First, it lies with the people themselves. They do not want to know the truth, so they surround themselves with people who are preaching their version of truth. As the years go by, their version of truth gets imbedded in their character, and they have no idea that they are deceived. **Don't listen to a pastor who only preaches what you want to hear.** Make sure you listen to one that preaches the uncompromised Word of God. This means there are times when their sermon might make you uncomfortable. As long as it is the truth of God's Word, go with the truth.

2 Peter 2:1
But there were also false prophets among the people, just as there will be false teachers among you. They will secretly introduce destructive heresies, even denying the sovereign Lord who bought them—bringing swift destruction on themselves.

Who are these people who are preaching destructive heresies

and denying the Lord? Unfortunately there are many today.

Jude 1:3–4
Dear friends, although I was very eager to write to you about the salvation we share, I felt compelled to write and urge you to contend for the faith that was once for all entrusted to God's holy people. For certain individuals whose condemnation was written about long ago have secretly slipped in among you. They are ungodly people, who pervert the grace of our God into a license for immorality and deny Jesus Christ our only Sovereign and Lord.

This is the group who preach that because of grace you can do anything you want. Don't deceive yourself and embrace this lie. We cannot say that we have not been warned.

It is also important to remember the seriousness of knowing, understanding, and interpreting Scripture accurately. This is paramount in guarding against deception.

Knowing the Scripture is very important, but it is not enough. The devil knows and quotes Scriptures too (Matthew 4:5–6). Believing, even though important, is not enough. The demons believe and tremble (James 2:19). Personal opinion or experience should never be the gauge one uses to validate the authenticity of God's Word.

Many are deceived because they violate exegetical principles to their own detriment, one being: **You cannot use one verse to create a doctrine.**

This violation has created the snake-handling churches. Members totally misinterpret Mark 16:18, so they pick up deadly snakes. Many have been bitten and have died. Even so, they continue this very foolish and dangerous practice. They overlook this verse in Luke 4:12, *"Jesus answered, It says: 'Do not put the Lord your God to the test.'"*

To clearly understand the verse this church is misinterpreting, God gave us clarity and an example in the book of *Acts 28:3– 6, "Paul gathered a pile of brushwood and, as he put it on the fire, a viper, driven out by the heat, fastened itself on his hand. When the islanders saw the snake hanging from his hand, they said to each other, 'This man must be a murderer; for though he escaped from the sea, the goddess Justice has not allowed him to live.' But Paul shook the snake off into the fire and suffered no ill effects. The people expected him to swell up or suddenly fall dead; but after waiting a long time and seeing nothing unusual happen to him, they changed their minds and said he was a god."*

Paul did not go looking for trouble. Trouble found him, but because he was walking in obedience to God, he suffered no ill effects from the snake. That is what the Scripture meant when it said that you shall pick up deadly snakes and they shall not harm you.

To avoid deception:

• Know the Word.

• Trust the Word.

• Study the Word.

• Meditate on the Word.

• Memorize the Word.

• Hide the Word of God in your heart.

Pray this prayer:

Father, open my eyes to the truth of Your Word. Help me to take the time to get to know and interpret Your Word correctly, which will keep me from being deceived. Amen.

Ephesians 1:18
I pray that the eyes of your heart may be enlightened in order that you may know the hope to which he has called you, the riches of his glorious inheritance in his holy people."

Key #21 Know Your Instrument: Know the Word

PARTIAL OBEDIENCE IS DISOBEDIENCE

One of the most disturbing stories of *partial obedience* leading to deception is found in 1 Samuel 15. God sent King Saul on a mission to completely destroy the Amalekites. Emphasis was placed on the word *"completely."* Saul went on the mission and left the Amalekite king and livestock alive. He partially obeyed. He failed to realize that partial obedience is disobedience.

After the mission was completed, Saul returned only to be confronted by the prophet Samuel, and a conversation ensued. What is troubling about their conversation is the length of time it took for Saul to realize that he was deceived.

Let us examine this conversation.

Saul: "I have carried out the Lord's instructions."

Samuel: "If you did, why am I hearing the bleating of sheep?"

Saul: "They killed everything but spared the best so they could sacrifice them to the Lord."

Samuel: "Why did you not obey the Lord and completely destroy everything?"

Saul: "I completely destroyed them and brought back Agag

125

their king, and the soldiers brought back the animals so we can sacrifice to the Lord."

Wow. Double wow. What would cause Saul to be this deceived? Saul's deception was so great he said, "I completely destroyed the Amalekites and brought back Agag their king."

If there is complete destruction, then there is nothing to bring back. Only a deceived person would make that kind of statement.

Samuel said, "Because you have rejected the word of the Lord, He has rejected you as king."

Once Saul heard those words, the lens of deception was lifted, *1 Samuel 15:24, "Then Saul said to Samuel, 'I have sinned. I violated the* Lord's *command and your instructions. I was afraid of the men and so I gave in to them.'"*

We need to have the ability to know when we are wrong.

Saul lacked this ability, and as a result of his deception, he lost the anointing on his life, lost his throne, and ultimately lost his life. We really need to guard against deception.

Key #22 Partial Obedience Is Disobedience

BE A DOER, NOT A HEARER ONLY

James 1:22
Do not merely listen to the word, and so deceive yourselves. Do what it says.

Over the years I have heard people say, "It's not that I don't know what to do. I just have not done it or have not made time to do it."

We can spend a lifetime acquiring knowledge, but if we fail to act upon the acquired information, we are only deceiving ourselves. *James 1:23–24: "Anyone who listens to the word but does not do what it says is like someone who looks at his face in a mirror and, after looking at himself, goes away and immediately forgets what he looks like."*

We have all heard people say:

I know if I exercise I will feel better.

I know I should quit drinking and smoking.

I know I should not be hanging out with these friends.

I know I should not text and drive.

I know I should be studying.

Keys To Avoiding Deception

I know, I know, I know.

If we know all these things, why the failure to act on our part?

It is time to declare war upon procrastination and say, "From this moment on, I am going to be a doer and not only a hearer. I will act upon the information I have acquired, and with God's help, my life will be transformed. This is the year of no more excuses."

Key #23 Be a Doer, Not a Hearer Only

BE HONEST WITH YOURSELF

Have you taken the honesty test?

Writing about honesty might seem trivial, but I have discovered that this is a major key in guarding against deception.

You can talk yourself into believing something that is not true simply because you have a habit of not being totally honest. The more you tell yourself this untruth, the more it becomes truth for you.

To avoid this deception, start with honesty.

I tell myself that if I am wrong, I am simply wrong. But how do I know I am wrong? It starts by always operating from a place of honesty. If you can come up with an excuse for every situation, you have officially entered the path to deception.

You will not arrive there overnight, but sooner or later you will get there.

I have met people who try to deceive everyone—even themselves. They fail to realize the importance of the honesty test.

If you cannot be honest with yourself, with whom can you be honest?

We can be deceived by others, but when we deceive ourselves, that is when it becomes really dangerous. To avoid deception, we have to be honest with ourselves.

At our home, we have many rules. One rule is the importance of telling the truth at all cost. Our children know that they can get away with many things, but lying is not one of them. Lying is almost like the unpardonable sin in the Brown household!

We had to establish a foundation of truth-telling because if a questionable situation arose, we needed to be able to trust our children's word. Even if they were guilty, as long as we knew the truth, we could help. Having this key paid dividends early on.

One day when our children were young, a friend came over to play. We could hear them having a great time upstairs. Very soon we heard a loud crash and we knew someone had broken something.

Our daughter's friend ran down the stairs and immediately blamed our daughter for breaking the object. Our daughter was not far behind. She ran up to me, held my hand, looked into my eyes and said, "Dad, I did not break it."

I then said to her friend, and everyone, "Our daughters know the consequences for lying, so if she said she did not break the object, I believe her."

When her friend realized how seriously we took lying, she confessed to breaking the object. I was so proud of our daughter because she saw first-hand the importance of laying a foundation of honesty. Honesty cannot be overstated and this showcased the importance of establishing principles of honesty.

Start by being honest with yourself. Take an introspective look at yourself and be totally honest. If you can't be honest with

KEYS TO AVOIDING DECEPTION

yourself, you will deceive yourself, and you will put yourself on a path that, sooner or later, will collide with reality.

This key is addressed in *Jeremiah 12:5–6, "If you have raced with men on foot and they have worn you out, how can you compete with horses? If you stumble in safe country, how will you manage in the thickets by the Jordan? Your relatives, members of your own family—even they have betrayed you; they have raised a loud cry against you. Do not trust them, though they speak well of you."*

The Scripture is saying that if you cannot beat another human in a race, why would you deceive yourself into believing you can outrun a horse?

If you cannot walk without stumbling on a straight path, what would make you believe that you can walk on a rugged path?

We can also apply this to faith and our own prayer lives.

If you cannot pray and believe that God will heal a headache, how can you believe God to heal cancer?

There are different levels of faith for different things. In Mark 9, the disciples could not cast a demon out of a sick child. Jesus got angry.

> Mark 9:19
> *You unbelieving generation, Jesus replied, how long shall I stay with you? How long shall I put up with you? Bring the boy to me.*

Why would Jesus get so angry? Obviously, something triggered His anger. I think what triggered His anger was the inability of the disciples to do what He knew they could do.

For clarity, we need to ask a few additional questions.

Was it God's perfect will to heal the boy? The answer is yes. If it was not God's perfect will, the boy would not have been healed.

What caused the boy not to be healed earlier? The disciples' lack of prayer and faith.

The disciples were concerned, and in private they asked Jesus a question in *Mark 9:28, "And when he was come into the house, his disciples asked him privately, 'Why could not we cast him out?'"*

Pay close attention to the answer Jesus gave them in *Mark 9:29*, "And he said unto them, this kind can come forth by nothing, but by prayer and fasting."

"This kind" means there are certain situations we will face when regular prayer will not resolve the problem. "This kind" means you need a greater level of prayer and faith to deal with. This also means that there are certain things that can only be accomplished by fasting and praying.

Taking the honesty test allows us to accurately assess our faith. Examine the proof of your faith. If there is no proof, be honest with yourself and ask God to help you so there will be proof. Our faith needs to have proof.

> 2 Thessalonians 3:2 (NIV)
> *And pray that we may be delivered from wicked and evil people, for not everyone has faith.*

> 2 Corinthians 13:5 (NIV)
> *Examine yourselves to see whether you are in the faith; test yourselves. Do you not realize that Christ Jesus is in you—unless, of course, you fail the test?*

132

James 2:20
But wilt thou know, O vain man, that faith
without works is dead?

Another aspect of the honesty test is to make sure we are not in *denial.*

Denial is a deadly disease that affects many people. Denial is one of the deadliest strains of deception.

The danger of denial is that many deceive themselves by believing that simply denying the issue will cause it to go away.

That is deception because whatever the issue is that you are denying, it will still be there whether you admit it or not. Get honest with yourself and deal with it. Don't deceive yourself by believing it will disappear simply because you denied it.

Taking the honesty test allows us to accurately diagnose our issues and then deal with them using Biblical solutions. As the saying goes, if you do not deal with your problems, your problems will deal with you. Many have subscribed to the belief that faith is denying the existence of a problem. That is not faith.

True faith is recognizing the problem and then saying what God says about the problem. No matter how impossible the situation looks, as long as you know you heard from God, just say what God says, and you will see the results.

It is like a person bleeding profusely, and the person says, "I am not bleeding."

Of course you are bleeding. Admit you are bleeding and then ask the Lord to stop the bleeding and heal the wound. The Scripture says in *James 5:14–15, "Is anyone among you sick?* *Let them call the elders of the church to pray over them and* anoint them with oil in the name of the Lord. And the prayer offered in faith will make the sick person well; the Lord will raise them up. If they have sinned, they will be forgiven."

The verse says, "Is any sick?" This is admitting people will get sick. It did not say, "Do not say you are not sick." It says, "Here is what you are to do if you are sick."

Key #24 Be Honest With Yourself

YOU WILL BE HATED, KNOW HOW TO RESPOND

Everyone wants to be loved. The need to be loved, accepted, cherished, and appreciated is a natural part of our true identity. At the same time, it is important not to deceive ourselves into thinking everyone is going to like us.

Get used to it. If you are truly going to follow Christ, people are going to hate you, as stated in *Mark 13:13, "Everyone will hate you because of me, but the one who stands firm to the end will be saved."*

Why are people going to hate you?

They are going to hate you because the message you will be preaching will go against popular culture. It won't be a feel-good-can-we-all-get-along message. There are pastors that the world loves simply because they are preaching a feel-good message. We are warned about this in Scripture.

2 Timothy 4:3–4
For the time will come when people will not put up with sound doctrine. Instead, to suit their own desires, they will gather around them a great number of teachers to say what their itching ears want to hear. They will turn their ears away from the truth and turn aside to myths."

The day you decide to preach the true message of Christ, prepare yourself for trouble.

The first sermon John the Baptist preached was not a politically correct sermon.

> Matthew 3:1–2
> *In those days John the Baptist came, preaching*
> *in the wilderness of Judea and saying, repent, for*
> *the kingdom of heaven has come near.*

What does *repent* mean? It means to turn from the *wrong* you are doing. That is not a politically correct word today.

The first sermon Jesus preached was not a politically correct sermon.

> Matthew 4:17
> *From that time on Jesus began to preach, repent,*
> *for the kingdom of heaven has come near.*

Do you see a pattern? We need to do the same.

The ministry of Jesus was not only in the church but was also in the marketplace. He went to where the people were and delivered His message. We need to do the same.

What did He teach in the public sphere? He taught on many subjects. Let us examine a few:

- He warns those who break the commandments and teaches others to do the same (Matthew 5:19).

- He warned that if our righteousness did not surpass the righteousness of the Pharisees we could not get into heaven (Matthew 5:20).

- He outlined rules for living (Matthew 5:21–32).

- He talked about murder, hell, taking people to court, lust, divorce, and adultery (Matthew 5:21-32).

- He raised the standard by saying that not only is the physical act of adultery wrong, but just looking lustily at a woman is similarly wrong (Matthew 5:27-28).

- He talked about swearing, loving our enemies, giving, prayer, fasting, and storing up treasures in heaven (Matthew 5:34-37).

- He talked about us not worrying but to seek God's kingdom first (Matthew 6:33). He warned about false prophets (Matthew 7:15).

Jesus sent the disciples to influence the culture, not vice versa. He also told them in Matthew 10:14–15, *"If anyone will not welcome you or listen to your words, leave that home or town and shake the dust off your feet. Truly I tell you, it will be more bearable for Sodom and Gomorrah on the day of judgment than for that town."*

This means do not try to force people to accept the gospel. Present the gospel in love, and if the people reject it, move on and go to another town.

He told them not to be afraid of those who can kill the body but cannot kill the soul. He said if we disown Him, He would disown us, too. He warned that His message would be very divisive. His message would cause family members to turn against each other.

Matthew 10:36
A man's enemies will be the members of his own household.

Jesus is calling us to a life of hardship—a life that goes into the marketplace with a very unpopular message. If we are true disciples of Christ, we will obey.

We have many voices today speaking, and many claim to be speaking for God. I am having major difficulty with many of the messages. Here is why.

The world is in trouble. When people are in trouble, they need to have an accurate assessment of their condition. The best thing we can do for anyone facing serious consequences, unless there is a major change, is to tell them the truth.

Where are the preachers telling the truth? I believe God is saying this to many pastors:

> Jeremiah 23:21–22
> *I did not send these prophets, yet they have run with their message; I did not speak to them, yet they have prophesied. But if they had stood in my council, they would have proclaimed my words to my people and would have turned them from their evil ways and from their evil deeds."*

It's time for all of us to wake up and give the nation the truth. We are in serious trouble, and unless we repent, judgment is just around the corner. Preaching this message will cause people to hate you, but get used to it. As long as God is pleased, you are good to go.

Key #25 You Will Be Hated, Know How to Respond

- Key #26 -

Count The Cost

Have you counted the cost?

You must *count the cost* before signing up to follow Christ.

The disciples had to count the cost and think carefully about what Jesus was calling them to do. We need to do the same. Let us take a look at a few verses and carefully examine the job description Jesus gave the disciples.

> Matthew 10:16–22
> *I am sending you out like sheep among wolves. Therefore be as shrewd as snakes and as innocent as doves. Be on your guard; you will be handed over to the local councils and be flogged in the synagogues. On my account you will be brought before governors and kings as witnesses to them and to the Gentiles. But when they arrest you, do not worry about what to say or how to say it. At that time you will be given what to say, for it will not be you speaking, but the Spirit of your Father speaking through you. "Brother will betray brother to death, and a father his child; children will rebel against their parents and have them put to death. You will be hated by everyone because of me, but the one who stands firm to the end will be saved.*

139

Pay close attention to some of the words Jesus used in this job description:

- You will be sheep among wolves. (This means you will be in danger.)

- You will be flogged.

- You will be arrested.

- Family members will betray you even to the point of death.

- You will be hated by everyone because of Him.

Wow! What a job description.

Following Christ is not an easy call, and it is imperative that we count the cost before we set sail to follow Him. One cost is that you will be hated by many people.

Get used to it. Once you sign up and are being used by God, expect opposition from the most unlikely sources.

God called Joseph to lead. Opposition came from his own brothers who hated him because of his dreams and sold him into slavery (Genesis 37).

Abel was hated and murdered by his brother Cain simply because God accepted Abel's sacrifice and not Cain's (Genesis 4).

David was called by God to lead. Opposition came from his own brothers who hated him, and one even accused him of being conceited and having a wicked heart.

> 1 Samuel 17:28 (NIV)
> *When Eliab, David's oldest brother, heard him*

speaking with the men, he burned with anger at him and asked, Why have you come down here? And with whom did you leave those few sheep in the desert? I know how conceited you are and how wicked your heart is; you came down only to watch the battle.

Interestingly, God said this about David *Acts 13:22 (NIV), "After removing Saul, he made David their king. He testified concerning him: 'I have found David son of Jesse a man after my own heart; he will do everything I want him to do.'"*

What an endorsement! "A man after My own heart." When you get that kind of endorsement from God, that's a recipe for success in life.

So who was David going to believe? His brothers or God? We all know the answer.

David was not deceived. He had counted the cost, so he knew he would be hated. He also knew all he had to do was allow God to define him and go with His definition.

Going with God's definition was critical for success in the life of David because later his friends turned on him and even talked about killing him. What a group of friends!

You really don't know who your lifelong friends are until your friendship gets tested.

Examine your friends' actions during the storm, and that will be a clear indicator of their loyalty to you. Loyalty does not mean approval. Loyalty means support during the storm. Loyalty means your friend will help you to navigate the storm even if you are wrong.

David was in major trouble. The families of the men he was

leading had been captured. They blamed him for allowing this to happen and talked about stoning him. This is a low place to be. The men he thought were his friends were talking about killing him *1 Samuel 30:6, "David was greatly distressed because the men were talking of stoning him; each one was bitter in spirit because of his sons and daughters. But David found strength in the Lord his God."*

On another occasion David's son Absalom became his enemy and was trying to kill him. During that time, one of his trusted advisors, Ahitophel, also turned against him.

With his friend turning on him, David wrote *Psalm 55:12–14, "If an enemy were insulting me, I could endure it; if a foe were rising against me, I could hide. But it is you, a man like myself, my companion, my close friend, with whom I once enjoyed sweet fellowship at the house of God, as we walked about among the worshipers."*

David experienced firsthand what Jesus would warn us about many years later.

Matthew 10:36
A man's enemies will be the members of his own household.

Jesus also gave us words of encouragement.

Matthew 5:11–12
Blessed are ye, when men shall revile you, and persecute you, and shall say all manner of evil against you falsely, for my sake. Rejoice, and be exceeding glad: for great is your reward in heaven: for so persecuted they the prophets which were before you.

Being hated by outsiders is terrible, but being hated by your own family is worse. How do you respond to a situation like this?

We respond by following the actions of David. The last part of 1 Samuel 30:6 says, *"But David found strength in the Lord his God."*

David responded by going to God and finding strength with God. We need to do the same.

Key #26 Count The Cost

DECISIONS
AND CONSEQUENCES

There are consequences attached to every decision that we make. The right decision will cost you, and the wrong decision will cost you. The only control we have is over the decision-making process. We have no control over the consequences. Make your decisions wisely.

As the saying goes, **"You make your decisions, but you do not pick the consequences."**

A major decision everyone needs to make is to follow Christ. It is important to know that once you do, a consequence will be that you gain enemies and lose friends. The gospel is offensive to unbelievers, and it will cause you to be hated, vilified, talked about, and called every name in the book.

Are you prepared for this?

Let us not deceive ourselves into thinking that we will not pay a price. There will be a price, and many times it is a big one.

> 2 Timothy 3:12–13
> *In fact, everyone who wants to live a godly life in Christ Jesus will be persecuted, while evildoers and impostors will go from bad to worse, deceiving and being deceived."*

1 Peter 4:12–14 (NIV)
Dear friends, do not be surprised at the painful trial you are suffering, as though something strange were happening to you. But rejoice that you participate in the sufferings of Christ, so that you may be overjoyed when his glory is revealed. If you are insulted because of the name of Christ, you are blessed, for the Spirit of glory and of God rests on you.

Matthew 5:11 (NIV)
Blessed are you when people insult you, persecute you and falsely say all kinds of evil against you because of me."

People can deceive themselves into thinking that making the right decisions will not have consequences; but many times they do.

- The right decision sent Joseph to prison (Genesis 39).

- The right decision sent Shadrach, Meshach and Abednego into the fiery furnace (Daniel 3).

- The right decision sent Daniel to the lion's den (Daniel 6).

- The wrong decision cost Saul the throne and ultimately his life (1 Samuel 15).

- The wrong decision cost Haman his life (Esther 7:10).

- The wrong decision claimed the lives of Eli, his sons, and his daughter-in-law all in the same day (1 Samuel 2:12–22).

- The right decision put the disciples in the middle of a storm (Mark 4:35–37).

Whose idea was it to go to the other side? Jesus. The disciples were simply walking in obedience to Jesus.

Mark 4:35
That day when evening came, he said to his disciples, "Let us go over to the other side.

Their obedience led them into the storm. Walking in obedience to God does not guarantee a problem-free life. As a matter of fact, it is usually the opposite. If you decide to follow Christ, get ready for trouble. Yes, there are great and incredible days for sure, but be prepared, because opposition will come from every side. Moses experienced this first hand. He was walking in obedience to God and encountered a storm.

Exodus 5:1
Afterward Moses and Aaron went to Pharaoh and said, "This is what the Lord, the God of Israel, says: 'Let my people go, so that they may hold a festival to me in the wilderness.'

The Lord gave Moses a message to deliver to Pharaoh, which he did. However the message created hardship. Let us examine Pharaoh's response to this message.

Exodus 5:6–9
That same day Pharaoh gave this order to the slave drivers and overseers in charge of the people: "You are no longer to supply the people with straw for making bricks; let them go and gather their own straw. But require them to make the same number of bricks as before; don't reduce the quota. They are lazy; that is why they are crying out, 'Let us go and sacrifice to our God.' Make the work harder for the people so that they keep working and pay no attention to lies."

What do you do when you are 100 percent sure you are following God's instructions and as a result of your obedience, things have gotten worse, and you are thrust into a major storm? You do what Moses did. You go back to the Lord.

> Exodus 5:22–23
> *Moses returned to the Lord and said, 'Why, Lord, why have you brought trouble on this people? Is this why you sent me? Ever since I went to Pharaoh to speak in your name, he has brought trouble on this people, and you have not rescued your people at all.'*

God comforted Moses by explaining that this was a part of a much bigger plan. Even though we do not understand the big picture, we just have to trust God that one day we will be able to say, "Now I understand."

You might ask, "If the consequence for making the right decision is pain, why make it?"

The simple answer is, **Temporary gain can lead to eternal pain, while temporary pain can lead to eternal gain.**

We give God thanks for His grace, mercy, patience, and long suffering with all of us. At the same time we need to understand that when we make a bad decision, His grace covers us when we ask for forgiveness, but consequences may yet occur. You can be forgiven but still have to live with the consequences of your actions.

To guard against deception we need to know the difference between self-inflicted wounds and wounds that are inflicted upon us for doing the right thing. Many times people suffer and are hated because of what they did, and not because they are standing up for Christ.

1 Peter 4:14–16
If you are insulted because of the name of Christ, you are blessed, for the Spirit of glory and of God rests on you. If you suffer, it should not be as a murderer or thief or any other kind of criminal, or even as a meddler. However, if you suffer as a Christian, do not be ashamed, but praise God that you bear that name.

Make sure your suffering passes the Biblical test. If it does not and you are suffering because you are the guilty party, pay restitution, apologize, and do the best you can to make it right.

We are all imperfect human beings, which means we will all make mistakes. There are mistakes, and then there are *mistakes.* We need to consider very carefully the decisions that we make because the consequences of our mistakes can be monumental.

God forgave Moses, but as a consequence he could not enter the Promised Land. Moses pleaded with God, but the consequences were irreversible, as explained in *Deuteronomy 3:23–26, "At that time I pleaded with the Lord: 'Sovereign Lord, you have begun to show to your servant your greatness and your strong hand. For what god is there in heaven or on earth who can do the deeds and mighty works you do? Let me go over and see the good land beyond the Jordan—that fine hill country and Lebanon.' But because of you the Lord was angry with me and would not listen to me. 'That is enough,' the Lord said. 'Do not speak to me anymore about this matter.'"*

David committed adultery and murder. God forgave him, but for the rest of his life he had to live with major consequences.

2 Samuel 12:9–10
Why did you despise the word of the Lord by

doing what is evil in his eyes? You struck down Uriah the Hittite with the sword and took his wife to be your own. You killed him with the sword of the Ammonites. Now, therefore, the sword will never depart from your house, because you despised me and took the wife of Uriah the Hittite to be your own.

David had made a bad decision and God forgave him, but as a consequence of his actions, the sword never departed from his house.

Wisdom dictates that we live in the now, but not at the expense of eternity. Make your decisions wisely because you will have no control over the consequence.

Key #27 Decisions and Consequences

FORGIVENESS

Forgiveness is one of the most powerful words in our vocabulary. Forgiveness is also a word that needs careful study. In order to avoid deception we need to know the difference between *forgiveness, reconciliation,* and *consequences.*

Forgiveness is a command. Even if the person who offends us never says he or she is sorry or asks for our forgiveness, we are commanded to forgive. We forgive not because we want to, but because we are all commanded by God to forgive.

> Matthew 6:14–15
> *For if you forgive other people when they sin against you, your heavenly Father will also forgive you. But if you do not forgive others their sins, your Father will not forgive your sins."*

> Luke 6:37
> *Do not judge, and you will not be judged. Do not condemn, and you will not be condemned. Forgive, and you will be forgiven.*

This means that forgiveness is not a suggestion. Forgiveness is a command.

Sometimes forgiving can be a very difficult task, and at times we wonder how many times we need to forgive. Peter wrestled with this as well and asked Jesus the appropriate question in *Matthew 18:21–22, "Then came Peter to him, and said, Lord, how oft shall my brother sin against me, and I forgive him? till seven times? Jesus saith unto him, I say not unto thee, Until seven times: but, Until seventy times seven."*

70 X 7 is 490 times. Why 490 times? I think Jesus listed that number simply to say just keep forgiving.

It is not easy to forgive, and many times it will push you to the limit. Still we must keep forgiving because if you don't, you will only affect yourself. As the saying goes, "Unforgiveness is like drinking poison and hoping the other person dies."

A few years ago I had the privilege of ministering at the Crystal Cathedral in California. While there I met Brooks Douglas who shared one of the most powerful stories of forgiveness I have heard.

Under false pretenses two men entered his home. They shot and killed his parents, assaulted his sister, and shot him. He and his sister miraculously survived and alerted the authorities.

Not long after, the men were caught and sentenced. One was given the death penalty and the other life in prison. Brooks witnessed the first killer's execution, and a few years later he visited the other gentleman in prison. The guy apologized saying that he was on drugs. He knew saying he was sorry would not bring his parents back, but for what it was worth he was sorry.

Brooks accepted his apology and before he left the prison, he felt the Lord say, "There is something you need to do."

Reluctantly, he held out his hand and said to the guy, "I forgive you," and he meant it from his heart.

151

He said the strangest thing happened after he released those words from his heart and mouth.

He started to cry uncontrollably and felt like poison was leaving his body. He said that for years he had a constant pain on his chest and that pain left immediately. He looked outside and the sky was blue, the leaves on the tree were green, and his vision changed with one act of forgiveness.

I was intrigued by his story and said, "Wow! You were shot, your sister was assaulted, and your parents were killed. At the same time by you offering the perpetrator of the crime true forgiveness, you were healed."

He said, "Yes, that's exactly what happened."

I took note and realized that offering someone true forgiveness is the catalyst for setting us free from the effects of this deadly poison called *unforgiveness.*

Quoting Lewis Smedes, "To forgive is to set a prisoner free only to discover that the prisoner was you."

We forgive not only to walk in obedience to God, but also to free ourselves from the bondage of carrying around the weight of this deadly poison.

Whether the person changes or not is irrelevant in forgiveness, and the truth is it's not always easy to forgive. Forgiveness is easy when there is behavior modification for sure, but without behavioral changes, it makes it more difficult. At the same time, even without behavior modification, we still need to forgive. Sometimes you have to forgive by faith and ask God to help you. It is also important to repeat that unforgiveness only hurts the person who refuses to forgive.

Does forgiveness mean that there are no consequences?

Are we being asked to live a life where no matter what the other person does, there are no consequences for their actions, because they are forgiven? Meaning, if a person lies, steals, or cheats—no matter what they do—we forgive them, and there are no consequences?

Does forgiveness mean we are a floor mat? People can walk over us all day and we just keep smiling, forgiving them, and leave the consequences up to God?

The answer is no, no, no.

The question that needs an answer is this, "What does true forgiveness look like?" True forgiveness happens internally, which results in an outward expression that demonstrates that the person has been forgiven. A person can be forgiven without knowing they are forgiven.

Forgiveness is based on *us*. Reconciliation is based on *us responding* to what the other person does. We can reconcile if we believe the other person's behavior has changed.

If they are truly sorry for what they did, they will take steps to demonstrate how sorry they are. At the same time, a person can be forgiven without reconciliation taking place.

Many have subscribed to the belief that they are not forgiven simply because there is no reconciliation, and there are consequences in place. Do not deceive yourself into thinking that because you are under God's grace, your mistakes will not have consequences. They do. You will be forgiven for sure, but there are still consequences in place.

Let us weigh our actions carefully, because the consequences of our mistakes can impact us for a lifetime.

Here are a few more examples of forgiveness and consequences:

Numbers 14:20–23
The Lord replied, 'I have forgiven them, as you asked. Nevertheless, as surely as I live and as surely as the glory of the Lord fills the whole earth, not one of those who saw my glory and the signs I performed in Egypt and in the wilderness but who disobeyed me and tested me ten times—not one of them will ever see the land I promised on oath to their ancestors. No one who has treated me with contempt will ever see it.'

Numbers 20:12
But the Lord said to Moses and Aaron, 'Because you did not trust in me enough to honor me as holy in the sight of the Israelites, you will not bring this community into the land I give them.'

God forgave Moses and Aaron, but the consequences were that they could not enter the Promised Land.

True forgiveness frees us to make the right decision because you never know what the future holds.

Many years ago while I was in high school, I overheard two guys talking about me. They did not know I was in an adjacent room hearing every word. What they were saying was not flattering, but I listened intently so I could gain wisdom.

My natural tendency would have been to confront them, but somehow I resisted the urge. It was more important to me to know their true feelings than believing a lie and deceiving myself. In spite of the hurt, I forgave them for what I heard and did not say anything to them. I could have written them off and avoided them at all cost, but I did not. We all make mistakes, and since God has forgiven us, we must forgive others as well.

A few months later we went to the beach. I was just learning to swim, and looking at the beautiful Caribbean Sea I got deceived. As a result of my deception, I jumped into the sea, believing the water was not deep.

As soon as I jumped in, I discovered the level of my deception. I kept sinking deeper and deeper. Finally I shot back to the top, and from there I started to scream for help.

I was about to drown, and guess who dove in to rescue me? The same guy I heard talking negatively about me earlier. By

God's grace he rescued me. The key to this story is you just

never know what the future holds, so never burn bridges behind you. A consequence of my forgiving him resulted in God using him to save my life.

Key #28 Forgiveness

HELP ME;
I NEED HELP!

Whenever the word *help* is uttered, everyone stops. They know someone is dealing with a situation that is beyond their capacity to handle and needs assistance.

Knowing when you need help and knowing when others need help is a key ingredient in guarding against deception.

Asking for help is not a sign of weakness but of strength. Asking for help means I have not deceived myself into thinking I am an island and can make it without any help.

Many people become hopelessly disillusioned because they deceive themselves into believing they don't need help. The truth is, we all need help.

If Jesus, the Son of God, knew He needed help, how much more should we?

> Matthew 26:38
> *Then he said to them, 'My soul is overwhelmed with sorrow to the point of death. Stay here and keep watch with me.'*

Jesus was facing the most monumental, consequential decision in the history of humanity, and He needed help. He was saying, "This is heavy. The burden is great. I am dying, and I need your support. Can you stay and watch with Me?"

Jesus knew he needed help and support. He went off to pray, and when He returned, He found His disciples sleeping. In anguish, He said, "Couldn't you men keep watch with me for one hour?"

Jesus was saying, "I am about to die and I need support. Can't you just watch with me for one hour?" What a lonely place this must have been. It is also important to say, "Can I help you?" to someone who needs help without knowing it.

Moses was a mighty man of God, but he still needed help.

In fighting the battle of Rephidim, victory did not rest on the battlefield. The battlefield was important, but victory rested with Moses' arms being raised in the air.

> Exodus 17:10–13
> *So Joshua fought the Amalekites as Moses had ordered, and Moses, Aaron and Hur went to the top of the hill. As long as Moses held up his hands, the Israelites were winning, but whenever he lowered his hands, the Amalekites were winning. When Moses' hands grew tired, they took a stone and put it under him and he sat on it. Aaron and Hur held his hands up—one on one side, one on the other—so that his hands remained steady till sunset. So Joshua overcame the Amalekite army with the sword.*

Being strong and doing the right thing does not mean you will not get tired and need help. Moses was strong and was doing the right thing, but being human, he got tired. Although he did not ask for help, his friends Aaron and Hur recognized that he needed help. They had him sit on a rock, and they held up his hands until victory had been won.

Who are the friends in your life who will hold up your hands, stand by you when the going gets tough, go cold so you can be warm, fast and pray for you until they see a breakthrough?

Who are the friends in your life you can call no matter how late the hour? If you do not have friends like these, start by investing in friendship. Start by first holding up the hands of others. Whose hands have you held up lately? Who have you gone hungry for so you could pray for them through their crisis?

If you have no such friends, become that person to others, and sooner or later, others will be helping you by holding up your hands in your time of need.

There are many who need their hands held up, and Scripture encourages this.

> Galatians 6:2
> *Bear ye one another's burdens, and so fulfil the law of Christ.*
>
> Romans 12:15
> *Rejoice with them that do rejoice, and weep with them that weep."*

Helping those in need is another key to guarding against deception. Many who have not helped anyone deceive themselves by looking for help in their time of need. When no help comes, they become angry and blame everyone but themselves.

Make a decision now to help others so you can be helped in your time of need.

Key #29 Help Me; I Need Help!

THE COMMON SENSE TEST AND THE FAITH TEST

Understanding the *common sense test* and the *faith test* are critical in guarding against deception.

For the believer, many times faith and common sense will collide. It is a war between the natural and the supernatural.

Over the years I have heard many stories, and my response has been, "This does not pass the common sense test." Other people hear the same stories and believe them. Other times I have heard amazing stories that defy human logic, but in my spirit the story passes the faith test. Others do not believe these stories.

How does one navigate this amazing dichotomy? We navigate by applying Key #1—Discernment, and by praying and operating with wisdom and faith. The truth is, faith makes no sense to the natural mind.

> 1 Corinthians 2:14
> *The person without the Spirit does not accept the things that come from the Spirit of God, but considers them foolishness, and cannot understand them because they are discerned only through the Spirit.*

As true believers, we are commanded to walk by faith. God is not making a recommendation or a suggestion. He is giving us a command, because He knows that we are going to need to understand this key in order to avoid deception.

God is telling us that if we are to please Him, it will require that we live in a state that at times makes no sense to our natural minds.

> Hebrews 11:6
> *And without faith it is impossible to please God, because anyone who comes to him must believe that he exists and that he rewards those who earnestly seek him.*

In 1 Kings 17, we find a fascinating story. In a time of famine, God sent Elijah to see a widow who was about to eat her last meal and die.

In the natural world one would ask, "Why would God tell Elijah that this woman would feed him until the famine was over, knowing that she was down to her last meal?"

In the natural realm, this would not pass the common sense test, but it passes the faith test. God knew Elijah's survival depended on Elijah hearing His voice and walking in complete obedience. He also knew that the woman's survival would be based on her putting her faith in the word of His servant Elijah.

God was going to use the woman's *natural* (her food) and combine it with Elijah's *supernatural* (his faith), and supply their needs for the duration of the famine.

To the natural mind this makes no sense, but Elijah knew the voice of God. He knew that in order to avoid deception and to survive, he needed to listen to the voice of God and then walk in faith, doing whatever God told him to do.

Faith is operating on another dimension that says, "My life is not based on what I can see, hear, or feel, but on what God has said."

Faith means leaving our comfort zone to operate on a level that sometimes defies human logic.

Faith makes no sense to the natural mind, and that is exactly how God wants us to live. *2 Corinthians 5:7 says, "For we walk by faith and not by sight."*

In the beginning of your faith journey, this might be very uncomfortable. It goes against everything our natural senses tell us, but with time we become more comfortable and also find it exciting. It becomes exciting because we know God is going to do something amazing; we just do not know how He is going to do it.

Noah built an ark expecting rain even though he had never seen rain. Why? Because God told him to build it (Genesis 6:13–22).

Abraham left his country and his people without knowing where he was going. Why? Because God told him to go (Genesis 12:1).

There are many stories that we can share about faith, but we will leave that for another book.

To guard against deception, we need to understand that God operates on a different system from the world's system. Our responsibility is to align ourselves with His system.

God's ways are not our ways, so we cannot use human logic to comprehend the things of God. The natural man without the Spirit cannot understand faith, and God is asking us now more than ever to learn to live by faith.

Here are some of the recommendations we find in Scripture that will cause faith and common sense to clash.

GOING INTO BATTLE
In 2 Chronicles 20, God said to send in the musicians first. I love the idea. A non-Christian would think this leader has lost his mind.

CRISIS OF LIFE AND DEATH
Esther declared a three-day period of fasting and prayer. A non-Christian would have serious thoughts about her mental faculties.

DEPRESSION
Send for an anointed musician.

Let us examine this last recommendation. In 1 Samuel 18, we find King Saul depressed and is being tormented by demons. Instead of recommending that he send for the best doctors, psychologist, or even a great psychiatrist, his servants recommended that he send for an anointed musician. What a recommendation. They understood the power of God's anointing on a musician.

Saul took their advice, and they found David. David was anointed by God, and each time he played the harp Saul got relief from depression. The demons left him.

If you are struggling with depression, get some worship music and saturate the atmosphere of your home with it. Very soon you will see a major difference. As the Scripture says, put on a garment of praise for a spirit of heaviness. The Scripture also says that God inhabits the praise of His people. The more you praise God, the more He dwells in your praise. Doing that will cause the devil to flee.

In another instance, a king needed advice. This king decided to seek out a true man of God for counsel (2 Kings 3:11). In today's society, many leaders would scoff at the idea of asking advice from a pastor. Let us examine in verse 15 what the man of God did when the king asked for his advice.

He brought in a musician to play. Very interesting.

The main point of this key is to make sure we are hearing God's voice clearly. God will show you what passes the common sense test and what passes the faith test.

Key #30 The Common Sense Test and The Faith Test

- KEY #31 -

SOWING AND REAPING

Proverbs 20:4
Sluggards do not plow in season; so at harvest time they look but find nothing.

Why would you look for a harvest if you did not sow?

This question can be applied to every area of life. Many times, students fail exams and in meeting with the teacher, one question normally comes up: Did you study?

A few times our children received a bad grade on an exam and were very disappointed. In comforting them we would ask: "Did you do the best you could?" Once they said "yes" we would tell them not to worry. All we ask is for you to do the best you can. When you know you have done your best by sowing the right seeds that in itself brings comfort.

The same applies to musicians who played in a recital that did not go well. The first question is: "Did you practice?"

It is also important to know that you can study and practice and still not get the grade or performance you desire. At the same time, knowing in your heart that you did the best you could makes a big difference.

I am sure you are asking the question. "What does sowing and reaping have to do with deception? This question has a lot to do with deception.

- You can't sow corn and when harvest time comes complain and say, "I wanted tomatoes." That's deception.

- You can't have alcohol in your house and be surprised when your children start to drink.

- You cannot use foul language and be surprised when your children begin to do the same.

- You cannot fill your children with a barrage of negativity and be surprised when they develop behavioral problems.

- You cannot cheat on your spouse and then be surprised when your children cheat on their spouse.

- You can't eat junk food all day and expect to be healthy.

> Galatians 6:7–9
> *Do not be deceived: God cannot be mocked. A man reaps what he sows. Whoever sows to please their flesh, from the flesh will reap destruction; whoever sows to please the Spirit, from the Spirit will reap eternal life. Let us not become weary in doing good, for at the proper time we will reap a harvest if we do not give up.*

Understanding the laws of sowing and reaping is very important in guarding against deception. Many times people reaping a negative harvest will try to give every plausible excuse for what is happening in their circumstance. However, in order to guard against deception we must ask ourselves one question: What kind of seed did I sow?

If you know in your heart you sowed good seed then you can

persevere. At the same time if you know you sowed negative seed, ask God to forgive you and in His mercy to change the outcome. God is a merciful God and with true repentance it is amazing how He can turn situations around.

Key #31 Sowing and Reaping

Keys For Living
PART FOUR

- *Key #32* -

BECOME A SERIAL LISTENER

Understanding the principles of listening in communication is pivotal in guarding against deception. This is an art that should be studied by all. Just because another person heard you say something that does not mean that they understood what you were saying. *Hearing* and *understanding* are two very different concepts.

I must confess that years ago—I mean many, many, many years, though I am sure my wife might say, *"years?"*—she would be talking to me. I would say "Yes, Dear," and "No, Dear." Halfway through her statements, she would stop and ask, "What did I say?"

I would respond jokingly. "Why are you asking me what you said? You know what you said." She would reply, "You were not listening, were you?" I would then admit I was not, even though I was saying "Yes, Dear," and "No, Dear." I was hearing, but not really listening.

On the other side many people are deceived because they fail to listen. They hear one sentence and then cut the person off before hearing the full context of what the other person is saying. This inevitably leads to wrong conclusions and deception. The Bible addresses this in *Proverbs 18:13, "He that answereth a matter before he heareth it, it is folly and shame unto him."*

Proverbs 29:20 (NIV)
Do you see a man who speaks in haste? There is more hope for a fool than for him."

Many times in written debates, I cut and paste the other person's words to make sure they know I am responding to their statements.

A good listener is one who responds by saying to the other person, "Help me to understand: is this what you are saying?" Then repeat what you thought you heard the person say.

If the person confirms you heard right, then you can comment from a position of wisdom, because you understand the full context of what the other person is saying.

Another key to guarding against deception is not only listening but also keeping a tight rein on our tongue. This simply means what, when, where, why, and how. We need to learn what to say, when to say, where to say, why we say, and how to say. Words are powerful, and we need to use them wisely.

The Bible has a lot to say about controlling our tongue.

James 1:19
My dear brothers and sisters, take note of this: Everyone should be quick to listen, slow to speak and slow to become angry.

Proverbs 17:27–28
The one who has knowledge uses words with restraint, and whoever has understanding is even-tempered. Even fools are thought wise if they keep silent, and discerning if they hold their tongues.

James 1:26
Those who consider themselves religious and yet do not keep a tight rein on their tongues deceive themselves, and their religion is worthless."

This art of listening should be studied by all.

Another aspect of listening we need to apply is listening in prayer. Prayer is a conversation, but for many people, it is a one-sided conversation. God wants a relationship, and in a relationship we listen to each other. For the most part, people tell God everything that is on their minds and never sit still long enough for the Lord to speak to them. I know I have been guilty of this, and I am sure many of you have too.

At home each evening after dinner we have family devotions and prayer. After everyone prays, we have a moment of silence to mediate and listen for the voice of the Lord. God wants to talk to all of us, but many times we are not listening. In quietness, it is amazing what we can hear. The silence can be deafening in the natural realm, but in the supernatural, God can be speaking loud and clear.

One morning after completing my time of prayer, I felt the Lord say to me, "You are not done praying yet." I went back to my prayer room and started to pray again. I then listened to find out what else I needed to hear. Immediately, one of our daughters called from college to ask for prayer because she was in pain and needed prayer. An hour later I got a call from another daughter on her way to school who said, "Dad, I think there is an accident because we have not moved for a long time." She was right. There was a very bad accident involving a student from her school and a truck. The student's car had flipped, but praise God miraculously the student survived with minor injuries. I drove by the scene and saw the car and I knew that a miracle had taken place that day.

There are times when God prompt us to pray, and we have no idea what we are praying for. The important thing for us to do is to simply obey the Lord and pray.

The main point I want to make here is simply this. A lack of clear communication can lead to major conflicts. Let us make sure we become *serial listeners* and double check to make sure that we are communicating clearly. This will help to guard us against deception.

Key #32 Become a Serial Listener

THE PRIORITY SCALE

What's your *priority scale?* Having a priority scale is of paramount importance in all our lives.

If you fail to make a priority scale, one will be made for you. I have a feeling you will not like the one that is made for you.

Ask yourself, "What are the priorities in my life right now?" For me they are:

1. God

2. Family

3. Ministry

Many people have put their ministries and their careers over their family, and that is a mistake. If you do not make your family a priority, do not deceive yourself and expect your family to make you a priority in the future.

A few years ago I was watching a very famous musician being interviewed on television. He made a statement that shocked me. He had just returned from a long tour and his wife shared a question their daughter had asked her. Their daughter asked, **"Mommy, where does Daddy live?"**

Ouch! What a question. Where does Daddy live?

As a result of that question, he decided to reshape his priorities.

I saw this interview before I got married, and vowed that would never happen to me. I have kept that vow. That is why I make sure I am home more than I am gone. Keeping this vow did not happen by accident. I had to be deliberate and purposeful. Many musicians go on three-month or six-month tours. I do not. There is only one *you,* and there are twenty-four hours in each day. We need to use them wisely. I have never heard of anyone on their deathbed say, "I wish I had done more tours or spent more time at the office."

Our number one priority needs to be God.

> Matthew 6:33
> *But seek ye first the kingdom of God, and his righteousness; and all these things shall be added unto you.*

What a powerful verse. God is telling us that seeking His kingdom should be our top priority. He knows that once we get our top priority in order, the rest of our lives will fall right into place.

Looking at the schedule I keep, I live by two sayings:

"I am too busy not to pray."

"Prayer! Don't leave home without it."

As a result, prayer is a priority for me. That is why I start each day in prayer. Make sure you know your priorities.

Key #33 The Priority Scale

Understanding Constructive and Destructive Criticism

Criticism—a word that has negative connotations—is an uncomfortable word that conjures up images of disappointment, disapproval, and discouragement.

No one likes to be criticized. At the same time, I have discovered that being criticized can have a positive impact on all our lives. Criticism can definitely be a great teacher.

Criticism falls into two categories: *constructive* and *destructive.* We need wisdom to know the difference. Many have been deceived because they believe that they are hated because they were criticized.

Wisdom dictates that everyone needs to be open to correction and criticism. At the same time, we have to walk carefully by knowing who we are first and then filter the criticism using the correct lens.

Over the years I have been called every name in the book, but I was not moved because I know who I am in Christ. If I had listened to some of the negative criticisms about myself, my self-esteem would have been destroyed. I refused to let my detractors define me.

When I am criticized, I ask myself one question: "Is there any truth to the criticism, regardless of who the person is?"

I then ask about the person's motives and examine their track record.

There are people who love to correct others; they get pleasure from putting others down. Once I had someone tell me to only listen to their criticism without responding. I told them no. If you are going to criticize someone, allow them to respond. What if your perception of the situation is wrong?

You criticism could be valid too, but with open dialogue wise people will know if you are telling the truth.

It is also important to know that *criticizing* and *confronting* are two very different concepts. Jesus tells us the right way to confront someone who has sinned against us. This is clearly outlined in *Matthew 18:15–17, "If your brother sins against you, go and show him his fault, just between the two of you. If he listens to you, you have won your brother over. But if he will not listen, take one or two others along, so that every matter may be established by the testimony of two or three witnesses. If he refuses to listen to them, tell it to the church; and if he refuses to listen even to the church, treat him as you would a pagan or a tax collector."*

1. The first step is to have a face to face meeting with the person.

2. If the person refuses to listen, take one or two people with you to confront them again.

3. If they still refuse, take it to the church.

4. After all this, if they refuse, walk away and leave them to their own demise. Continue to love and pray for the person though.

Make sure your criticism builds instead of tears down.

Proverbs 12:18
Reckless words pierce like a sword, but the tongue of the wise brings healing.

Ephesians 4:29
Do not let any unwholesome talk come out of your mouths, but only what is helpful for building others up according to their needs, that it may benefit those who listen.

Key #34 Understanding Constructive and Destructive Criticism

Do Not Try to Defend
the Indefensible

There are people who can explain just about any situation. They can put a spin on any negative situation without admitting wrongdoing. That is very dangerous because this always leads to deception.

Wisdom dictates that if it is wrong, we simply say it is wrong. This does not mean condemning a person. It means admitting what they did was wrong and then applying a Biblical solution based on forgiveness.

A woman was caught in adultery and brought to Jesus in *John* 8:3–11:

> *Then the scribes and Pharisees brought unto him a woman taken in adultery; and when they had set her in the midst, they say unto him, Master, this woman was taken in adultery, in the very act.*
>
> *Now Moses in the law commanded us, that such should be stoned: but what sayest thou?*
>
> *This they said, tempting him, that they might have to accuse him. But Jesus stooped down, and with his finger wrote on the ground, as though he heard them not.*

So when they continued asking him, he lifted up himself, and said unto them, He that is without sin among you, let him first cast a stone at her.

And again he stooped down, and wrote on the ground.

And they which heard it, being convicted by their own conscience, went out one by one, beginning at the eldest, even unto the last: and Jesus was left alone, and the woman standing in the midst.

When Jesus had lifted up himself, and saw none but the woman, he said unto her, Woman, where are those thine accusers? Hath no man condemned thee?

She said, No man, Lord. And Jesus said unto her, Neither do I condemn thee: go, and sin no more.

We all need to study the response of Jesus and learn from the example that He set.

First, He dealt with the hypocrisy of her accusers. They brought the woman to Jesus. Why did they bring only the woman? Where was the man? Then He dealt with her by saying, "Go thy way and sin no more."

David admitted that he had sinned with Bathsheba when the prophet confronted him. He did not make excuses or try to put a spin on his mistakes. He accepted full responsibility.

2 Samuel 12:13
Then David said to Nathan, 'I have sinned against the Lord.'

He never gave excuses for his behavior. His first words were, "I have sinned against the Lord." We need to do the same.

Many times people quote *Matthew 7:1, "Do not judge, or you too will be judged."*

I often hear that quote when another person wants to stop the other person from calling sin, sin. They invoke that verse to call for *tolerance.*

We cannot judge people's hearts or motives because we are not privy to their internal thought processes. At the same time, there is a reason we are given clear guidelines in Scripture.

Religious tolerance is not found in the Bible. Let us examine a few examples. Jesus did not say He is *one* way to God. He said that He is the *only* way. *John 14:6, "Jesus answered "I am the way and the truth and the life. No one comes to the Father except through me."* That is not religious tolerance. Jesus is saying He *is* the only way.

1 John 5:11–12, "And this is the testimony: God has given us eternal life, and this life is in his Son. He who has the Son has life; he who does not have the Son of God does not have life." Jesus is saying that without Him, you do not have life.

When the critics challenged Jesus about His divine nature He said in *John 8:55, "Though you do not know him, I know him. If I said I did not, I would be a liar like you, but I do know him and keep his word."* He called them liars (which they were). That is not religious tolerance.

He goes a step further in John 8:44, *"Ye are of your father the devil, and the lusts of your father ye will do. He was a murderer from the beginning, and abode not in the truth, because there is no truth in him."*

Jesus answered His critics by telling them they were of their father the devil. That is definitely not religious tolerance. Jesus never taught religious tolerance. He told us to call people to repentance.

Jesus never told us to tolerate false doctrine. He told us to warn people about the coming judgment in order to save them from a eternity without God.

Titus 3:10
Warn a divisive person once, and then warn them a second time. After that, have nothing to do with them.

Ezekiel 33:8
When I say to the wicked, 'O wicked man, you will surely die,' and you do not speak out to dissuade him from his ways, that wicked man will die for his sin, and I will hold you accountable for his blood. But if you do warn the wicked man to turn from his ways and he does not do so, he will die for his sin, but you will have saved yourself.

Key #35 Do Not Try to Defend the Indefensible

- KEY #36 -

DEVELOP AN INSATIABLE APPETITE FOR THE TRUTH

Today, more than ever, we need a spirit of wisdom and discernment to decipher the truth. People have found new ways to hide and obstruct the truth. Just because something is posted online, in the newspapers, or has been reported by the major TV or radio networks does not mean it is true.

Many times it takes years to prove to someone that what they heard and believed was not the truth.

There are parody websites writing fiction because they believe it is funny. When did it become acceptable to write incendiary and inflammatory false information that defames the character of innocent people and believe it is funny?

Anyone who believes this is funny is walking in pure deception. Many lives have been severely affected by the lies of these websites. Once they wrote that a major minister had become an atheist. This created an international crisis for this pastor who had to do major damage control.

This explains the need for all of us to seek truth and make sure we verify the information we accept as truth. In the past I have been accused of being too cautious here. Some feel that when they tell us something, we need to believe it—no questions asked.

This is wrong thinking. I tell my friends that when I tell them something, there is nothing wrong with checking it out to make sure my information is correct. As a matter of fact, I strongly encourage that.

Many times the mainstream media disseminate false information, and then they recant. Suppose I give you information that's not correct and you start passing it around, saying, "I got it from my friend, and that's good enough for me." That would lead to deception.

I have seen many stories published in the media and very shortly after, the networks recant the story. Sadly, on many of these occasions people only hear the original story, and they never hear the recanted version.

There are companies that make millions of dollars because they have the ability to manipulate the internet in such a way that the negative is hidden and only the positive appears on the first few pages. This can be good if the negative is based on untruth. At the same time it can be very bad if the negative is the truth, and people need to know.

Truth is a powerful word, and the search for truth has been going on for years. Pilate was searching, too, and he asked Jesus a profound question in *John 18:38, "Pilate saith unto him, what is truth?"*

What a question. *What is truth?*

Pilate did not wait for an answer, but earlier, Jesus answered that question for His disciples in *John 14:6, "Jesus answered, 'I am the way and the truth and the life. No one comes to the Father except through me.'"*

Jesus was saying, "I am the truth; the truth is wrapped up in who I am."

Once we find Jesus, we will find eternal truth; truth that sets us free. This truth stands on its own and will speak for you.

> 3 John 1:1
> *Demetrius is well spoken of by everyone—and even by the truth itself. We also speak well of him, and you know that our testimony is true.*

You know you are on the right path when you are well-spoken of by the truth itself. The truth will defend you.

Make sure you are not fighting the truth and do not know it. That is deception, *as 2 Timothy 3:8, "Just as Jannes and Jambres opposed Moses, so also these teachers oppose the truth. They are men of depraved minds, who, as far as the faith is concerned, are rejected."*

You are walking in pure deception when you oppose the truth and do not know it. As imperfect human beings, we can analyze situations the wrong way. Perception is not necessarily reality. Many times we hear a story, and the person sharing his or her perspective sounds very convincing. How do we know if their perspective is the correct one?

> Proverbs 18:17 (NIV)
> *The first to present his case seems right, till another comes forward and questions him."*

This means we need to exercise caution and use wisdom to analyze each situation carefully. We have opinions, facts and evidence, and the truth. **Make sure your opinion and the truth do not clash.** That's a recipe for deception which can lead to disaster.

The good news about the truth is that it is always going to be there—whether we admit it or not. If it is the truth, sooner or later it will come to light. Focus on what is true.

It is also important to understand that the truth does not set anyone free. It is the truth *that you know* that sets you free. This is supported in John 8:32, which says, *"Then you will know the truth, and the truth will set you free."*

Everyone who knows me well knows whenever I go into a debate, I generally start with two questions.

1.   How do you come to truth?

2.   What litmus test do you use to come to a conclusion that you have the truth?

I start with those questions because for me that opens a window into the person's thought process. We might still disagree for sure, but once I understand your thought process it helps me. Finding truth should be of paramount importance in all our lives. You would hate to build your life's foundation on a lie and then one day find out you were deceived.

Truth stands on its own. This means it is true for all people at all times and in all places. It's an entity that exists all on its own, and even if someone disagrees, that would have no bearing on the fact because it is true.

One truth we know for sure is that we exist. The philosopher Descartes said, "I think, therefore I am." He bases the truth of his existence on the fact that he thinks. The problem I see with that perspective is, how about a person in a vegetative comatose state lacking the ability to think? Does that person exist?

If someone tells you that you do not exist, does that mean you do not exist? To avoid deception, focus on truth. People who focus on truth are not easily deceived.

Key #36 Develop an Insatiable Appetite for the Truth

Do Not Leave Untruth or Half-Truth Unchecked

Half-truth or untruth can do untold damage to one's character. Many times it takes years to recover from character assassination.

If you know someone has a negative opinion of you based on untruth or half-truth, and you are in a position to change that and you don't, that is a recipe for disaster.

This is dangerous because people process situations through the lens of their own experience. When the person has no point of reference because you decided you don't care what they think, they are going to use their past experiences to assess the situation and define you.

Not only that, they might be asked to comment about you in the future and because you failed to give an alternate viewpoint, the negative untruth or half-truth about you gains traction and will spread like wildfire.

Do not say, "I do not care what they think of me," because that is deception.

> Proverbs 22:1
> *A good name is rather to be chosen than great riches, and loving favor rather than silver and gold."*

Proverbs 12:22
The Lord detests lying lips, but he delights in men who are truthful."

Key #37 Do not Leave Untruth or Half-Truth Unchecked

- KEY #38 -

NONNEGOTIABLES

What are the nonnegotiables in your life?

Is there anything in your life that would cause you to say, "No matter what laws are passed, no matter what threats are made, no matter how many friends I lose, even if it costs me my life, I will never compromise on this because this is a nonnegotiable?"

In Scripture, we find many examples of people with nonnegotiables.

King Nebuchadnezzar built a statue and commanded everyone to bow down and worship it. Failure to comply with this command would result in the death penalty.

Shadrach, Meshach, and Abednego decided that this was a nonnegotiable, so they refused to worship the king's statue. On hearing this, the king got angry and summoned them, as described in *Daniel 3:13–18:*

> *Furious with rage, Nebuchadnezzar summoned Shadrach, Meshach and Abednego. So these men were brought before the king, and Nebuchadnezzar said to them, "Is it true, Shadrach, Meshach and Abednego, that you do not serve my gods or worship the image of gold I have set up? Now when you hear the sound of*

the horn, flute, zither, lyre, harp, pipe and all kinds of music, if you are ready to fall down and worship the image I made, very good. But if you do not worship it, you will be thrown immediately into a blazing furnace. Then what god will be able to rescue you from my hand?

Shadrach, Meshach and Abednego replied to him, "King Nebuchadnezzar, we do not need to defend ourselves before you in this matter. If we are thrown into the blazing furnace, the God we serve is able to deliver us from it, and he will deliver us from Your Majesty's hand. But even if he does not, we want you to know, Your Majesty that we will not serve your gods or worship the image of gold you have set up.

They were saying, "King, this is a nonnegotiable for us. No matter what threats you make, no matter what laws you pass, even if you give us the death penalty, we will never serve your god." The king was so upset he threw them into a fiery furnace, but God rescued them. (For the rest of the story, read Daniel 3:19–30.)

Daniel also had a nonnegotiable. He would only pray to the true and living God. His enemies wanted him dead, so they devised a plan to trap him, because they knew this was a nonnegotiable in his life.

Daniel 6:5
Finally these men said, 'We will never find any basis for charges against this man Daniel unless it has something to do with the law of his God.'

Their devious plan worked, and they tricked the king into signing into law the death penalty for anyone who refused to pray to him. The king did not know that they were setting a trap for Daniel. What Daniel's enemies failed to realize is that only a deceived person would believe they can fight against God and win. Daniel was not moved by the new law because this was a nonnegotiable for him. As a result, he prayed just like he had done before.

> Daniel 6:10
> *Now when Daniel learned that the decree had been published, he went home to his upstairs room where the windows opened toward Jerusalem. Three times a day he got down on his knees and prayed, giving thanks to his God, just as he had done before.*

Soon Daniel was caught praying and the penalty of death under the law was imposed on him. He was thrown into a den of hungry lions. God saw Daniel's nonnegotiable, heard his prayer, and sent His angels to rescue him. The next day, the king went to see if Daniel's God had been able to save him.

> Daniel 6:20–23
> *And when he came to the den, he cried with a lamentable voice unto Daniel: and the king spake and said to Daniel, O Daniel, servant of the living God, is thy God, whom thou servest continually, able to deliver thee from the lions? Then said Daniel unto the king, O king, live for ever. My God hath sent his angel, and hath shut the lions' mouths, that they have not hurt me: forasmuch as before him innocency was found in me; and also before thee, O king, have I done no hurt. Then was the king exceedingly glad for him, and commanded that they should take Daniel up out of the den. So Daniel was taken up out of the den, and no manner of hurt was found upon him, because he believed in his God.*

Daniel's enemies should have studied the lessons of Key #31 on sowing and reaping; specifically,

> Galatians 6:7–9
> *Do not be deceived: God cannot be mocked. A man reaps what he sows."*

They had sown, and now it was time to reap.

> Daniel 6:24
> *At the king's command, the men who had falsely accused Daniel were brought in and thrown into the lions' den, along with their wives and children. And before they reached the floor of the den, the lions overpowered them and crushed all their bones.*

Mordecai had a nonnegotiable in his life, too. He would only bow down to the true and living God. Everyone in the nation bowed down and paid homage to Haman, but Mordecai would not bow because that was a nonnegotiable for him.

> Esther 3:2
> *All the royal officials at the king's gate knelt down and paid honor to Haman, for the king had commanded this concerning him. But Mordecai would not kneel down or pay him honor.*

Even under pressure from the royal officials, he refused to bow.

> Esther 3:3–4
> *Then the royal officials at the king's gate asked Mordecai, 'Why do you disobey the king's command?' Day after day they spoke to him but he refused to comply. Therefore they told Haman*

about it to see whether Mordecai's behavior would be tolerated, for he had told them he was a Jew.

Peer pressure will cause you to want to compromise on your belief system, but if your nonnegotiables are truly nonnegotiables, you will never bow no matter how much pressure is placed on you. Your nonnegotiables will sustain you when pressure comes. **A nonnegotiable that's deeply embedded in your character will never respond to any form of pressure.**

Haman was told about Mordecai's behavior so he formulated a plan to kill him. Soon, Mordecai learned that he had been given the death penalty and upon learning this, his response is worth noting.

> Esther 4:1
> *When Mordecai learned of all that had been done, he tore his clothes, put on sackcloth and ashes, and went out into the city, wailing loudly and bitterly.*

Deep distress overwhelmed him, and he went out weeping and wailing. With all the tears and fears, bowing down to Haman was not an option because that was a nonnegotiable. Bowing down would mean compromising his integrity. This infuriated Haman even more.

> Esther 5:9
> *Haman went out that day happy and in high spirits. But when he saw Mordecai at the king's gate and observed that he neither rose nor showed fear in his presence, he was filled with rage against Mordecai.*

Haman was so upset with Mordecai's nonnegotiable, he

formulated a plan not only to kill Mordecai, but to destroy his family and entire race. He tricked the king into allowing him to do this and then spread the word so Mordecai would know he was a dead man for refusing to acquiesce to his demands. Haman was walking in full-blown deception, and as a result he violated two major keys without realizing what would be the consequences.

First, he followed the wrong advice. In Key 15 we talked about the importance of having the right advisors. He consulted his wife and friends who were supposed to be great advisors, but look at the advice they gave him.

> Esther 5:14
> *Then said Zeresh his wife and all his friends unto him, Let a gallows be made of fifty cubits high, and to morrow speak thou unto the king that Mordecai may be hanged thereon: then go thou in merrily with the king unto the banquet. And the thing pleased Haman; and he caused the gallows to be made.*

Second, he encountered Key 31: The Law of Sowing and Reaping. Haman went to the king to get permission to hang Mordecai on the gallows.

> Esther 6:4
> *And the king said, Who is in the court? Now Haman was come into the outward court of the king's house, to speak unto the king to hang Mordecai on the gallows that he had prepared for him.*

Haman arrived at the right time because the king was in the process of honoring Mordecai, the person he wanted to kill.

The queen also was in the process of exposing Haman's vile

plot. Haman's timing could not have been any better. Esther explained the plot against her and her people. When the plot was exposed, the king became angry and wanted to know who was responsible for such a diabolical plot.

> Esther 7:6–10
> *And Esther said, The adversary and enemy is this wicked Haman. Then Haman was afraid before the king and the queen. And the king arising from the banquet of wine in his wrath went into the palace garden: and Haman stood up to make request for his life to Esther the queen; for he saw that there was evil determined against him by the king. Then the king returned out of the palace garden into the place of the banquet of wine; and Haman was fallen upon the bed whereon Esther was. Then said the king, Will he force the queen also before me in the house? As the word went out of king's mouth, they covered Haman's face. And Harbonah, one of the chamberlains, said before the king, Behold also, the gallows fifty cubits high, which Haman had made for Mordecai, who spoken good for the king, standeth in the house of Haman. Then the king said, Hang him thereon. So they hanged Haman on the gallows that he had prepared for Mordecai. Then was the king's wrath pacified.*

Haman thought he was building the gallows for Mordecai who had a nonnegotiable in his life, but the reality was he was building it for himself. Be very careful how you sow because you do not want to be surprised at harvest time.

What are the nonnegotiables in your life? Make sure they are time-tested, variable and backed up by the Word of God.

Key #38 Nonnegotiables

USE THE RIGHT LENS

What is the right lens?

A few years ago I was driving and discovered I could not see the street signs clearly. Shortly after that I was fitted with glasses. One night I had a concert and was driving without a GPS. Realizing I could not see the signs clearly, I put on my new glasses. I was amazed at the clarity. I could read all the signs, and I was seeing definitions I had not seen before.

I discovered that by simply putting on my new glasses with the right lens, I could see clearly. My wife tried to use the same glasses but could not because they were not the right lenses for her. It's amazing the clarity one is able to see once they use the right lenses.

So, what are the right lenses in guarding against deception? The right lenses are lenses that say it is not *who* is right or wrong—it is *what* **is right.**

There are many different lenses people use to help in drawing their conclusions. Wisdom dictates that we should not filter situations through who is right and who is wrong. We must use the right lens instead.

In the journey of life, many judgment calls have to be made on conflicting situations.

There are two popular sayings: "Don't believe your lying eyes," and "If someone tells you who they are, believe them." Many times people are deceived because they fail to believe both.

The worst form of deception is picking the wrong side and then unknowingly defending the guilty because you filtered the situation using the wrong lens.

Successful Christian counselors never talk about who is right and who is wrong. They talk about what is right. They try to establish biblically what is right and then filter both parties through that lens. The truth will prove who is right.

There are two sides to every argument, so it is important to hear both sides before drawing a conclusion. I quoted this verse before but it is worth quoting again. *Proverbs 18:17, "The first to present his case seems right, till another comes forward and questions him."*

We all want to believe the best about everyone, but if the signs are there that something is wrong, we should never dismiss the signs. Many people get deceived because they say, "This is my friend, so I am going to support him or her no matter what." That's a recipe for disaster.

You can support another person by not being a willing party to their demise.

If you choose one side over the other because of favoritism, that inevitably leads to wrong conclusions and deception.

As true Christians, we should never filter situations using the lens of favoritism. Many have said blood is thicker than water, meaning that because the person is a relative you need to take their side. I could not disagree more.

Truth is an entity all to itself, which means it stands on its own.

If our relatives are wrong, they are simply wrong.

In situations like these, Jesus would say to all of us, "Search for truth and stick with it." Many tragedies have happened, and people inevitably say, "How could this happen? I had no idea. I never saw this coming."

Interestingly, after the dust has settled and they take an honest look at the evidence, they say the signs were there all along, but they just never saw it or chose not to see it. Others will say they just could not believe what they were seeing. Do not filter situations through who is right and who is wrong. Filter them through the lens of what is right.

Key #39 Use the Right Lens

Don't Dwell
on The Past

Isaiah 43:18
Forget the former things; do not dwell on the
past. See, I am doing a new thing!

God is encouraging all of us to forget the past. The past can be
a very dangerous place, and dwelling there can lead to
deception because one's perspective of a present reality, is not
based on current truth.

As the saying goes, "Perception is not necessarily reality."

You can look at a situation and become deceived because you
are filtering the situation using past history. Remember: **God**
never consults your past to determine your future.

2 Corinthians 5:17
Therefore if any man be in Christ, he is a new
creature: old things are passed away; behold, all
things are become new.

The past is the past. If you have confessed your past failures,
regrets, and mistakes to the Lord, they are gone forever.

Philippians 3:13–14
Brothers and sisters, I do not consider myself yet
to have taken hold of it. But one thing I do:

Forgetting what is behind and straining toward what is ahead, I press on toward the goal to win the prize for which God has called me heavenward in Christ Jesus.

If anyone needed to forget the past, it was Paul. Listen to his story.

Acts 26:9–11
I too was convinced that I ought to do all that was possible to oppose the name of Jesus of Nazareth. And that is just what I did in Jerusalem. On the authority of the chief priests I put many of the Lord's people in prison, and when they were put to death, I cast my vote against them. Many a time I went from one synagogue to another to have them punished, and I tried to force them to blaspheme. I was so obsessed with persecuting them that I even hunted them down in foreign cities."

With this kind of past, how do you move forward?

You move forward by first confessing your sins and leaving them at the cross.

The devil will try to talk you into doing maintenance on your past mistakes and live a life of constant regret. Do not let him. Confess your sins and then move on. Do not allow the devil to torment you with past mistakes, which are forgiven.

At home we tell our kids: **Do not complain about what you allow.**

Of course, the devil is going to do everything in his power to discourage you. Fight back. Do not allow him to discourage you.

When he reminds you of your past, just quote this passage to him, *"As far as the east is from the west, so far has he removed our transgressions from us"* (Psalm 103:12).

The past is the past. Do not dwell on it.

A few years ago I was arranging a song on my keyboard. After many days of work, I decided to save the song. The keyboard was new, so I was not familiar with all the settings. Somehow I hit the wrong button and when I tried to reload the song, there was nothing. I mean *silence.*

I panicked and contacted the keyboard company. The tech representative came on the phone, and I started by saying, "Please promise me you will say yes to my request."

He said he would do his best, but could not promise. I was desperate so I pleaded again: "Just promise me you will be able to."

With that, he asked a few questions and then zeroed in on one button.

He asked, "Did you press that button?"

I said, "Yes," and he said, "Oh no."

I pleaded, "Please tell me you can help."

He said, "I am so sorry, but that button deleted everything. It's gone forever."

I said, "What do you mean it is gone forever? Are you saying it is gone, done, finished, caput, and can't be recovered?"

He said, "Yes."

I pleaded, "There must be something we can do to retrieve the information," but he said no. I discovered in a hurry that no matter what I tried, even if I cried, got angry, hit my head against a wall for being foolish, or used a sledge hammer to break the keyboard, it was gone forever. There was nothing I could do to retrieve the information. It was gone for good.

I learned a very important lesson that day. I also remembered it is the same with God. When He deletes our sins, they are gone forever.

When you give your life to Christ, your slate is wiped clean. Everything you have done wrong in the past is now gone: deleted, washed away, and gone forever.

Oh what a relief that is!

Imagine living your life knowing all the wrong things you have done are forgiven. That alone should encourage everyone to become a Christian.

Think about this. By making the most important decision of your life to follow Jesus Christ, all your past mistakes are deleted.

If you have hidden sins that were never dealt with, until you confess and deal with them you will be deceiving yourself. If you do not deal with your problems, sooner or later your problems will deal with you. Do not deceive yourself by thinking that your hidden problems will not resurface. Until they are dealt with, they will always be there. Many times they will be exposed at the worst possible time. Deal with your problems now. Do not deceive yourself by thinking they have gone away simply because you have ignored them. As *Proverbs 28:13 says, "Whoever conceals their sins does not prosper, but the one who confesses and renounces them finds mercy."*

Confession of sin is very important, so if you are dealing with past regret and want your sins totally forgiven right now, and I mean *right now,* just say this prayer:

> Dear God,
>
> I know I am a sinner. Please forgive me for all my sins. I believe that Jesus died and rose again, paying the penalty for my sins. Please come into my heart and make me new. From this moment on I promise to live for you. Give me the strength to live for you each day. In the name of Jesus I pray. Amen.

If you have prayed that prayer and meant it, then everything that you have done wrong in the past is totally gone—I mean, totally deleted like I deleted the song from my keyboard. Now live in victory. For more information on being a Christian turn to Key 44.

Key #40 Don't Dwell on the Past

- KEY #41 -

BE CONSISTENT

Living a consistent life allows others to get an accurate picture of who you truly are. Consistency creates stability, trustworthiness, and a foundation that is rock solid.

Being consistent produces a life where people won't have to guess about your views on clear-cut issues.

A few years ago I was talking to a gentleman from the FBI. He mentioned a story in which he was preparing someone to give a testimony in court. When he spoke to the person about going over their testimony they said, "Don't worry about what I have to say. The truth comes out the same way every time."

What a powerful statement. "The truth comes out the same way every time."

I have had conversations with people and at times I wonder which person will be showing up because they are never consistent. One day they have one position, and the next day it is a different one. Others say they speak out of both sides of their mouth. The problem with people who double-speak is sooner or later they will deceive themselves without knowing it.

Adding to the confusion is the perspective of the hearers. The hearers have to decipher the message they heard, and on occasion they might be asked to comment on the message bearer.

A person who double-speaks might be placed in a certain category, and I am sure they will not like the category in which they are placed in.

Playing the double-speak game is very dangerous and should be avoided at all cost. In order to avoid this kind of deception, let us agree to be consistent.

> James 1:8
> *A double minded man is unstable in all his ways.*

People who know me well know my views are not rehearsed. They are deep-rooted, and you will not hear me say one thing today and something else tomorrow.

I also know as people mature, their views can change, and there is nothing wrong with that. What is wrong is when you are talking to a person and you have no idea where they stand on clear-cut issues because they are consistently inconsistent. Be consistent. Do not be a double-minded person.

Key #41 Be Consistent

- *Key #42* -

DON'T BE A SPIRITUAL
BLIND GUIDE

Jesus made a very strong statement that offended a few people. His disciples who wanted to protect him brought it to His attention. Notice the statement and the response of Jesus to the disciples.

First the statement.

> Matthew 15:7–9
> *You hypocrites! Isaiah was right when he prophesied about you: 'These people honor me with their lips, but their hearts are far from me. They worship me in vain; their teachings are merely human rules.'*

This is not a feel-good-can-we-all-get-along statement.

His disciples then brought it to His attention.

> Matthew 15:12–14
> *Then the disciples came to him and asked, "Do you know that the Pharisees were offended when they heard this?" He replied, "Every plant that my heavenly Father has not planted will be pulled up by the roots. Leave them; they are blind guides. If the blind lead the blind, both will fall into a pit."*

Ouch!!!

Interestingly, Jesus did not say, "I am sorry they were offended. Let me go and apologize." He doubled down and added to His statement by saying that they were *blind guides.*

Are you a blind guide?

If you believe because of grace you can live in sin, you are a blind guide. If you can use the Bible to justify and promote sin, you are a blind guide. If you do not care about the poor or less fortunate, you are a blind guide. If you can go to a strip club, feel comfortable, fit right in and do not feel convicted, you are a blind guide. If you can feel comfortable with your friends who use drugs and foul language around you, you are a blind guide. If the world loves you, you could be a blind guide.

Get used to this truth. If you are going to be a true follower of Christ you will be hated. It is important to note that a Biblical worldview and a secular worldview can never be reconciled. They are polar opposites.

Jesus said we are supposed to be the light of the world.

> Matthew 5:14
> *Ye are the light of the world. A city that is set on an hill cannot be hid.*

Light dispels darkness not vice versa.

Jesus never changed His message to attract sinners. Sinners were attracted to Him because of His miracles and His message.

Notice the response of these people when they encountered Jesus.

Luke 19:8
But Zacchaeus stood up and said to the Lord, 'Look, Lord! Here and now I give half of my possessions to the poor, and if I have cheated anybody out of anything, I will pay back four times the amount.'

He was convicted and made amends.

The woman at the well in John 4:29, "Come, see a man who told me everything I ever did. Could this be the Messiah?"

Let us examine the conversation between Jesus and the woman:

John 4:16–18
He told her, 'Go, call your husband and come back.' 'I have no husband,' she replied. Jesus said to her, 'You are right when you say you have no husband. The fact is, you have had five husbands, and the man you now have is not your husband. What you have just said is quite true.'

That is not a feel-good message to win someone over according to some modern-day theology.

After Jesus spoke to the people who had brought to him a woman caught in adultery, He said to her in *John 8:11, "Go now and leave your life of sin."* The King James Version says, *"Go thy way and sin no more."*

After Jesus healed a lame man, He said to him in *John 5:14, "See, you are well again. Stop sinning or something worse may happen to you."*

Jesus was told about the terrible things Pilate had done.

Notice His response to the people who brought the message.

Luke 13:3
I tell you, no! But unless you repent, you too will all perish.

The world has changed. The prophecy listed in 2 Timothy 4:3 is taking place right now, *"For the time will come when people will not put up with sound doctrine. Instead, to suit their own desires, they will gather around them a great number of teachers to say what their itching ears want to hear."*

Are you a blind guide? Deception is being a blind guide and not knowing it.

If you are, repent before it is too late. God is not going to change His Word for any of us. We need to make sure our belief system lines up with His Word.

Key #42 Don't Be a Spiritual Blind Guide

ANSWER LIFE'S MOST IMPORTANT QUESTIONS

What are life's most important questions?

I believe they are questions that have eternal significance; questions where there is no room for error. Here are a few that I believe should be on everyone's priority list.

1. Is there a God? We addressed this in chapter 2.

2. Is truth relative or absolute?

3. Do all roads lead to God? (Relative truth)

4. Is there just one way to God? (Absolute truth)

5. How do I know that Christianity is the right way?

6. What is my purpose for being on earth?

7. What happens when we die?

8. Who gets to heaven, and what is the criteria for getting there?

Many people approach these questions from this standpoint, "No one knows what happens, and I don't care." People who take the "I don't care" approach are only deceiving themselves.

The truth is, we are all going to die one day. If it means taking a lifetime to answer these questions, we should.

What if *you* are wrong? What if *I* am wrong? I decided to answer the *what if I am wrong* question years ago.

My conclusion was and still is, If I am wrong I have lost nothing. I would have lived a good life, done the best I could, and tried to make the world a better place.

What if you are wrong? What are the consequences if you deceive yourself and fail to address these very important questions?

Many people say there is no afterlife and no hell. At the same time, Jesus spent His life warning us about the danger of hell. *Matthew 5:30, Matthew 8:12, Matthew 10:28, Mark 9:47, Revelation 21:7–8,* and many more.

The question we need to address is, **why would Jesus waste His time warning us about the danger of a nonexistent place?**

What happens if you live your life denying the existence of God, only to die and find out you had deceived yourself and there really is a God?

Being sincere, even though wrong, will not cause God to look upon us favorably.

The truth is, unless Jesus returns, we know with absolute certainty that we will all die one day. The question is, "What happens next?" This is a question I implore everyone to answer. Do not leave that question unchecked.

Key #43 Answer Life's Most Important Questions

- KEY #44 -

ARE YOU A REAL CHRISTIAN?

Who is a Christian?

What is the test that one uses to determine if a person is a real Christian?

If we ask the Rastafarians who the real Rastafarians are, they can tell you. This would be the same for a Muslim, Buddhist, Hindu, Atheist, Agnostic, and all the other religious or nonreligious groups. Why does it seem like all the other groups can clearly articulate who their believers are, while many Christians have difficulty answering this question?

Many have said all one needs to do is say they are a Christian, and that is good enough. Others believe because they were born in a "Christian" nation or into a Christian family, that automatically makes them a Christian. This is far from the truth. As the saying goes, "Being born in a garage does not make you a car." It is also important to note that nations are not Christians—people are.

Is a Christian a person who prays a prayer and lives any way that they want to live?

If someone tells you they love God, but they love the things that God hates, are they a true Christian?

If someone tells you they love God but they hate their brother, are they a true Christian?

If someone tells us that they are a Christian but they contradict what Jesus said and taught, are they a Christian?

So who is a true Christian, and what evidence can one look at to confirm that the person is truly saved?

The song *"We are one in the Spirit"* tries to answer this question by saying, "They will know we are Christians by our love."

This is backed up in 1 John 4:8, *"Whoever does not love does not know God, because God is love."*

This means that if you do not love, you do not know God.

A true Christian is one who knows and loves God. If you love God, you will walk in obedience to His Word. His Word tells us to love our fellow man in *1 John 4:20, "If anyone says, 'I love God,' yet hates his brother, he is a liar. For anyone who does not love his brother, whom he has seen, cannot love God, whom he has not seen."*

A true Christian is one who has confessed and repented of their sins.

A true Christian is one who has accepted the free gift of salvation found in Jesus Christ only.

The word *Christian* is used three times in the New Testament, Acts 11:26; 26:28 and 1 Peter 4:16. Followers of Jesus Christ were first called "Christians" in Antioch (Acts 11:26) because their behavior, activity, and speech were like Christ. The word *Christian* literally means, "belonging to the party of Christ" or a "follower of Christ."

A true Christian should have a consistent demonstration of the fruit of the Spirit in his or her life. True Christianity is accompanied by behavior modification and a clear demonstration of fruit in the life of the new believer.

If there is no proof, what would one use to make a determination that this person is truly a Christian?

If you say you are a Christian and nothing has changed in your life after accepting Christ, how can you say you are a real Christian? *2 Corinthians 5:17 tells us, "Therefore if any man be in Christ, he is a new creature: old things are passed away; behold, all things are become new."*

The Scripture says you are a new creature. So if you are a true Christian, people will see proof of change.

There are many people telling the world that they are Christians without proof. Here are two very troubling passages we all need to keep in mind:

> Titus 1:16
> *They claim to know God, but by their actions they deny him. They are detestable, disobedient and unfit for doing anything good.*

> Matthew 23:15
> *Woe to you, teachers of the law and Pharisees, you hypocrites! You travel over land and sea to win a single convert, and when he becomes one, you make him twice as much a son of hell as you are.*

These are serious verses. Jesus is saying these people are deceived. They believe they are saved, but they are not. They are in danger of hell and do not know it. That is the ultimate deception.

When it comes to our eternal destiny, there is no room for error.

A gentleman attended my Bible study one night. At the study, he declared he was a Christian, a Muslim, and a Buddhist. He said by definition he was all of the above.

By definition, *Christian* means follower of Christ, *Muslim* means one who submits his or her will to Allah, and a *Buddhist* means one who is enlightened.

According to this man's beliefs, by strict definitions, he was all of the above. I explained to him that this was not possible.

His beliefs were problematic on many fronts, and to prove this, I had to ask some additional questions, and his answers confirmed my suspicions.

1.   He did not believe the miracles stated in the Bible.

2.   He did not believe that Jesus had a virgin birth.

3.   He believes Jesus' biological father was Joseph.

4.   He believes that the Bible has been tampered with.

5.   He believes Jesus did not die for our sins.

6.   He believes Jesus did not rise from the dead.

7.   He believes that there are many paths to God.

I was in shock because I don't know how anyone having these views can say they are a Christian. Not only that, I find it fascinating that he found a few churches that support his views.

I explained to him that what he and his church were doing was preaching a different gospel. The Bible warns us about a different gospel.

Galatians 1:6–8
I am astonished that you are so quickly deserting the one who called you by the grace of Christ and are turning to a different gospel which is no gospel at all. Evidently some people are throwing you into confusion and are trying to pervert the gospel of Christ. But even if we or an angel from heaven should preach a gospel other than the one we preached to you, let him be eternally condemned.

These are strong words by Paul. I don't want anyone to be condemned, but that's what Paul is saying in defense of the true gospel. Paul is asking the church how we can possibly turn to a different gospel now? The question everyone needs to answer is, **What is the true gospel?**

The Bible answers this question.

1 Corinthians 15:3–5
For what I received I passed on to you as of first importance: that Christ died for our sins according to the Scriptures, that he was buried, that he was raised on the third day according to the Scriptures, and that he appeared to Peter and then to the Twelve.

That is the gospel—pure and simple, Jesus dying, being buried, rising from the dead, and paying the penalty for our sins. How can a person who does not believe Jesus died and rose from the dead be a true Christian? If Jesus did not die and rise from the dead, we are all in serious trouble.

Paul addresses this important question.

> 1 Corinthians 15:14–18
> *And if Christ has not been raised, our preaching is useless and so is your faith. More than that, we are then found to be false witnesses about God, for we have testified about God that he raised Christ from the dead. But he did not raise him if in fact the dead are not raised. For if the dead are not raised, then Christ has not been raised either. And if Christ has not been raised, your faith is futile; you are still in your sins. Then those also who have fallen asleep in Christ are lost. If only for this life we have hope in Christ, we are of all people most to be pitied.*

Praise God, Jesus did rise from the dead, and there is enough proof of His resurrection for us to be confident.

I then asked a question. "Would you knowingly die for a lie?"

He said, "No." I would not, either. No one would knowingly die for a lie.

All of the apostles of Jesus except John were executed because they would not recant their position. They went to their graves declaring that the teachings of Jesus are true and that He rose from the dead. If their testimony was a farce, one of them would have renounced his stand to save his life. They never did. They went to their death declaring Jesus was the true Messiah and had risen from the dead.

It's also important to note that many secular sources record the life of Jesus. Historians like Flavius Josephus, the Jewish Talmud, Thallus, and Phlegon, all mention Jesus. The history of Jesus is recorded in other sources besides the Bible.

All true Christians believe that Jesus died and rose again. All true Christians know they can have assurance of eternal life based on their accepting the free gift of salvation, found in Jesus. Have you accepted this free gift?

You might be a member of a church for many years but deep down you know you have never accepted Jesus as your Lord and Savior. If not, you can do so now. I know I listed this prayer in chapter 40 but it is such an important one, I am compelled to list it again.

Just pray this prayer:

> Dear God,
>
> I know I am a sinner. Please forgive me for all my sins. I believe that Jesus died and rose again, paying the penalty for my sins. Please come into my heart and make me new. From this moment on I promise to live for you. Give me the strength to live for you each day. In the name of Jesus I pray. Amen

If you prayed that prayer and meant it, welcome to the family of God. All your sins are now washed away. You will wonder what to do next.

1. Get a Bible. Start by reading the book of John.

2. Make it a priority to pray every day. Prayer is simply a conversation between you and God. Just talk to God every day, and I promise it will change your life.

3. Tell others about your experience, and tell them about the life they can also have with Jesus.

4. Find a good church that preaches the uncompromised

Word of God. There are many churches, but not all are preaching the true gospel. If you find a church that preaches something that contradicts the Bible, leave that church immediately. We covered this verse before but it's worth repeating again.

2 Timothy 4:3
For the time will come when people will not put up with sound doctrine. Instead, to suit their own desires, they will gather around them a great number of teachers to say what their itching ears want to hear.

5.   Study the Bible on what it means to really worship God. Become a true worshipper.

6.   Volunteer to work at your church in some capacity.

Key #44 Are You a Real Christian?

- KEY #45 -

FINAL EXAM

Life is a journey, and on this journey we take many exams. I thought for years that there would be a final exam at the end of our lives but I was wrong. Life is not preparation for a final exam.

Life is the final exam.

When you die there is nothing you can do about this exam. All you are doing is waiting for the results to come in. The results of this exam are sealed until judgement day.

> 2 Corinthians 5:10 NIV
> *For we must all appear before the judgment seat of Christ, so that each of us may receive what is due us for the things done while in the body, whether good or bad.*

In school after taking final exams, many students anxiously wait to see the results. For some the results will determine if they graduate or not. It is the same for all humanity. We are all taking our final exams right now. When we die we are simply waiting for the results to be read at judgement day.

How are you doing with your final exam? Take a look and grade yourself as best as you know how. Keep in mind that God's grading system is quite different than the worlds. Make sure you use God's grading system. At the end of life, our grade will not be based on how we answered the questions after death. They are going to be based on how we answered them now.

Think about that, every action you take now is being graded and placed in a book.

> Revelation 20:12-13 NIV
> *And I saw the dead, great and small, standing before the throne, and books were opened. Another book was opened, which is the book of life. The dead were judged according to what they had done as recorded in the books. The sea gave up the dead that were in it, and death and Hades gave up the dead that were in them, and each person was judged according to what they had done.*

You might be wondering about the questions we will be judged on? Here they are.

FINAL EXAM

1. Are you born again? Keep in mind that going to church does not make you born again.

    > John 3:3
    > *Jesus replied, Very truly I tell you, no one can see the kingdom of God unless they are born again.*

2. Do you believe all roads lead to God?

    > John 14:6
    > *Jesus answered, I am the way and the truth and the life. No one comes to the Father except through me.*

All roads do not lead to God. Jesus is saying that you cannot get to the Father except through Him. Are you trying to get to God without Jesus?

3. There is a list of people that the Scripture says will not be going to heaven. Let us examine ourselves to make sure we do not fall into any of the categories listed. If you do, then determine to do something about it. Eternity hangs in the balance.

> Revelation 21:8
> *But the cowardly, the unbelieving, the vile, the murderers, the sexually immoral, those who practice magic arts, the idolaters and all liars— they will be consigned to the fiery lake of burning sulfur. This is the second death.*

> 1 Corinthians 6:9–10
> *Or do you not know that wrongdoers will not inherit the kingdom of God? Do not be deceived: Neither the sexually immoral nor idolaters nor adulterers nor men who have sex with men nor thieves nor the greedy nor drunkards nor slanderers nor swindlers will inherit the kingdom of God.*

Let's examine ourselves to make sure we are not in any of those categories.

4. Is your name written in the Lamb's book of life?

> Revelation 21:27
> *Nothing impure will ever enter it, nor will anyone who does what is shameful or deceitful, but only those whose names are written in the Lamb's book of life.*

KEYS TO AVOIDING DECEPTION

5.   Did you feed the hungry?

6.   Did you quench the thirst of the thirsty?

7.   Did you take care of strangers?

8.   Did you provide clothes for those who needed clothing?

9.   Did you visit the sick?

10. Did you visit those in prison?

> Matthew 25:31–36, 41–46
> *When the Son of man shall come in his glory, and all the holy angels with him, then shall he sit upon the throne of his glory: And before him shall be gathered all nations: and he shall separate them one from another, as a shepherd divideth his sheep from the goats: And he shall set the sheep on his right hand, but the goats on the left. Then shall the King say unto them on his right hand, Come, ye blessed of my Father, inherit the kingdom prepared for you from the foundation of the world: For I was an hungred, and ye gave me meat: I was thirsty, and ye gave me drink: I was a stranger, and ye took me in: Naked, and ye clothed me: I was sick, and ye visited me: I was in prison, and ye came unto me.*

> Matthew 25:41–46
> *Then shall he say also unto them on the left hand, Depart from me, ye cursed, into everlasting fire, prepared for the devil and his angels: For I was an hungred, and ye gave me no meat: I was thirsty, and ye gave me no drink: I was a stranger, and ye took me not in: naked, and ye*

clothed me not: sick, and in prison, and ye visited me not. Then shall they also answer him, saying, Lord, when saw we thee an hungred, or athirst, or a stranger, or naked, or sick, or in prison, and did not minister unto thee? Then shall he answer them, saying, Verily I say unto you, Inasmuch as ye did it not to one of the least of these, ye did it not to me. And these shall go away into everlasting punishment: but the righteous into life eternal.

Taking this passage at face value, many have subscribed to the belief that all they need to do is good works—taking care of the poor—and then they will inherit eternal life.

That is not the case.

Doing good works is very important. If you are a true Christian, good works will follow. Good works is a natural byproduct demonstrating that one is truly saved. It is like jumping into a swimming pool and getting wet. Getting wet is a natural outcome of jumping into a pool.

All true Christians take care of the poor, feed the hungry, take care of the sick, and visit those in prison, but doing good works alone will not get you into heaven. If doing good works could get us into heaven, Jesus would not have to die for our sins. There are atheists, with no regard for God, doing good works.

It's also important to note that **perfect people do not go to heaven. Forgiven people do.**

Let's take those questions seriously.

Revelation 22:12 NIV
Look, I am coming soon! My reward is with me,

*and I will give to each person according to what
they have done.*

Revelation 22:14–15 NIV
*Blessed are those who wash their robes, that
they may have the right to the tree of life and
may go through the gates into the city. 15
Outside are the dogs, those who practice magic
arts, the sexually immoral, the murderers, the
idolaters and everyone who loves and practices
falsehood.*

If you fall into any of those categories, I have good news. You
can get out of that category. All you have to do is confess your
sins. Tell God something He already knows. Ask Him to
forgive you and to take the reins of your life. For the rest who
won't make a decision, there are two camps in which people
will be placed.

Camp 1

Matthew 25:34
*Come, you who are blessed by my Father; take
your inheritance.*

Camp 2

Matthew 25:41
*Depart from me, you who are cursed, into the
eternal fire prepared for the devil and his angels.*

One group will enter into eternal life, and the other group will
face eternal death.

Which one will you be in?

Key #45 Final Exam

CONCLUSION
Written by: Natalie Brown

At the heart of this discussion lies an honest conversation with God. Deception is both a difficult and daunting concept to understand. With that being said, it is still one we must observe with whole hearted conviction through the lens of Scripture as Christ followers. In choosing to not only observe but put into the practice the keys listed throughout this book, we offer ourselves space to more clearly understand the word of God for the truth that it is. It is my hope that the lessons found within these chapters continue to speak to us with both clarity and conviction.

I've watched this book evolve over the course of the past few years. What began as a small set of lessons laid upon the heart of my dad has now turned into the gift we each hold within our hands. This topic is so critically important because it speaks to the heart of faith versus fear, the known versus the unknown, our own understanding and God's revelation.

We are at a critical time in history and as the Church we must be equipped to stand against deception. Christ must continue to go before us in our earthly pursuit of Him and His Kingdom.

James 1:5-6 states, *"If any of you lacks wisdom, you should ask God, who gives generously to all without finding fault, and it will be given to you. But when you ask, you must believe and not doubt, because the one who doubts is like a wave of the sea, blown and tossed by the wind."*

My prayer is that God will give you wisdom to understand the words within these pages, which will lead you to a more honest conversation with Him.

I'd like to conclude with a prayer for us all:

Lord, teach us to cling to your truth and your truth alone. Continue to shield our hearts and minds from that which is not from you. Teach us to love your wisdom and your word. Remind us of your faithfulness in the midst of our own desires. May you use these words to further strengthen our faith. Teach us to listen to your voice which will guard us against deception. As we close this book may we walk away with a deeper understanding of who you are and how we are called to follow you. Amen.